Natural Resource Condition Assessment

Whitman Mission National Historic Site

Natural Resource Report NPS/UCBN/NRR-2009/118

Jack Bell
Northwest Management, Inc.
PO Box 9748
Moscow, ID 83843

Dustin Hinson
AMEC Earth and Environmental, Inc.
11810 North Creek Parkway N
Bothell, WA 98011

June 2009

U.S. Department of the Interior
National Park Service
Natural Resource Program Center
Fort Collins, Colorado

The Natural Resource Publication series addresses natural resource topics that are of interest and applicability to a broad readership in the National Park Service and to others in the management of natural resources, including the scientific community, the public, and the NPS conservation and environmental constituencies. Manuscripts are peer-reviewed to ensure that the information is scientifically credible, technically accurate, appropriately written for the intended audience, and is designed and published in a professional manner.

Natural Resource Reports are the designated medium for disseminating high priority, current natural resource management information with managerial application. The series targets a general, diverse audience, and may contain NPS policy considerations or address sensitive issues of management applicability. Examples of the diverse array of reports published in this series include vital signs monitoring plans; monitoring protocols; "how to" resource management papers; proceedings of resource management workshops or conferences; annual reports of resource programs or divisions of the Natural Resource Program Center; resource action plans; fact sheets; and regularly-published newsletters.

Views, statements, findings, conclusions, recommendations and data in this report are solely those of the author(s) and do not necessarily reflect views and policies of the U.S. Department of the Interior, NPS. Mention of trade names or commercial products does not constitute endorsement or recommendation for use by the National Park Service.

This report is available from the Natural Resource Publications Management Web site (http://www.nature.nps.gov/publications/NRPM) on the Internet.

Please cite this publication as:

NPS 371/100128, June 2009

Contents

Figures

Tables

Executive Summary

The Natural Resource Condition Assessment (NRCA) program is designed to give the managers of Whitman Mission National Historic Site (WHMI) a point in time assessment of their natural resources. The program is designed to better understand and evaluate existing data concerning the condition of natural resources within and adjacent to the park. Both aquatic and upland habitats will be assessed and treated separately along with identifying threats and stressors; such as invasive species, water pollution, and land development; that pose a significant negative impact to WHMI's natural resources. Information gained from this report will form the basis for development of actions to reduce and prevent impairment of WHMI's natural resources and assist in the development of Resource Stewardship Plans.

The study identified a project area composed of 3-6th level Hydrologic Unit Code (HUC) watersheds with a 2 km buffer. All available geographical information (GIS) was acquired for the project area to create an ArcGIS Map Project File and Geodatabase. This product is used to make maps and for analysis of geographically based data. All site-specific data was compiled in GIS. Upland data is available in the digital database and the aquatic data is attached to this report. Maps and pictures were provided for each upland and aquatic sample site along with a description of the site and assessment of condition.

The upland sites sampled were 7 vegetation restoration management units (VRM) originally established in 1984. All were evaluated based on the ecological site, as defined by soil type and an established reference condition (Pellant 2005). Each sample site received a 5 level rating for condition in 3 landscape attributes; soil stability, hydrologic function, and biotic integrity. Overall, the soil stability and hydrologic function attributes were in good condition, rated none-slight departure from reference conditions. The biotic integrity attribute in several sites were in poor condition, rated slight-moderate departure. The main reason for the poor condition was attributed to past land use practices and the presence of noxious weeds.

Mill Creek and Doan Creek were selected for site-specific condition status assessments. Sites selected for evaluation were assessed using the "proper functioning condition" (PFC) riparian assessment methodology developed by the Bureau of Land Management for lotic, flowing water, (Prichard et al. 1998). Both aquatic sites were rated "Functional-At-Risk." The poor condition of most sites was attributed to one or more of the following threats; water level fluctuations, invasive riparian species, recreational use, fine sediment accumulation, and/or land use.

The development of private lands adjacent to the park is a known threat/stressor to the park's natural resources. The population of Walla Walla County has increased by 4.6% over the past seven years. However, parcel level data was not available to predict specific areas of concern and recommendations are to pursue acquisition of these records through cooperation with the County. Noxious weeds currently pose the greatest threat to WHMI natural resources.

In WHMI 14 noxious or invasive species have been either listed as important or physically inventoried the past 24 years. Of these only 2 were not identified in reports reviewed for this report. WHMI has identified 6 of these as species of concern and are targeted in there management activities. Over 40 noxious weed species have been identified by the Walla Walla

County Noxious Weed Control Board as high priority for eradication and control. Only 2 species have been identified in the park. Accurate mapping of surrounding lands would allow WHMI staff to be more strategic in the noxious weed management by being prepared for possible new invaders and cooperating on control of existing species.

Climate in the Pacific Northwest is predicted to have warmer, wetter winters with an increase of 3.1° F. by 2030 coupled with a 5% increase in precipitation (Mote et al. 2005). Precipitation is predicted to come more in the form of rain with smaller snow packs with seasonal flows shifting markedly toward larger winter and spring flows and smaller summer and autumn flows. The 43 sub-basins in the Columbia River basin have their own sub-basin management plans for fish and wildlife but none comprehensively addresses reduced summertime flows under climate change. Possible impacts to ecosystem processes, communities, and/or species can only be address through future natural resource planning based on the predicted climate changes.

Of the 21 threats/stressors (6-natural, 15-human-caused) examined 12 could pose potentially high impact to one or more of the major resources/processes; soils, hydrologic, biotic, and air. Many of these are not directly manageable by park staff, such as the natural disturbances and changes that occur outside the park boundary. Several can be directly managed by the park, like invasive plants, and visitor use. Others, like rural development, can have their impact moderated or mitigated through planning and cooperation with other resource management agencies and private land owners.

Overall, WHMI has many future challenges to achieve the stated desired goal for resource management (NPS 2000). Results of this report should assist park managers in identifying when, where, and how to improve management practices, justify additional resources, and prepare for the changes in environment that will directly impact WHMI natural and cultural resources.

Acknowledgements

We wish to begin by thanking Roger Trick, Natural Resource Manager at Whitman Mission National Historic Site, for his time and courteous help in all stages of the project. Mr. Trick was extremely helpful providing us with valuable background information and was very open in sharing his many years of knowledge about the site. Gerald Ladd of AMEC provided great assistance in field work. Vaiden Bloch, GIS Specialist, with Northwest Management, Inc. was invaluable in preparing the Geodatabase and map project files. We would like to thank the many staff at Northwest Management, Inc. for their edits and insightful comments on the manuscript, especially Diane Corrao, Administrative Manager. Finally, we are very thankful for all the support and help from Lisa Garrett, NPS Upper Columbia Basin Network, and Jason Lyon, NPS Nez Perce National Historical Park. They had the vision to develop and implement this project and the professionalism and dedication to guide it to completion.

Introduction

Purpose and Scope

The mission of the National Park Service is "to conserve unimpaired the natural and cultural resources and values of the national park system for the enjoyment of this and future generations" (National Park Service 1999) To uphold this goal, the Director of the NPS approved the Natural Resource Challenge to encourage national parks to focus on the preservation of the nation's natural heritage through science, natural resource inventories, and expanded resource monitoring (National Park Service 1999). Through the challenge, 270 parks in the national park system were organized into 32 inventory and monitoring networks.

The Upper Columbia Basin Network (UCBN) consists of nine widely separated NPS units located in western Montana, Idaho, eastern Washington, and central Oregon. Parks of the Upper Columbia Basin Network include: Big Hole National Battlefield (BIHO), City of Rocks National Reserve (CIRO), Craters of the Moon National Monument and Preserve (CRMO), Hagerman Fossil Beds National Monument (HAFO), John Day Fossil Beds National Monument (JODA), Lake Roosevelt National Recreation Area (LARO), Minidoka Internment National Monument (MIIN), Nez Perce National Historical Park (NEPE), and Whitman Mission National Historic Site (WHMI).

As part of the Natural Resource Challenge, the NPS Water Resources Division received an increase in funding to assess natural resource conditions in national park units. Management oversight and technical support for this effort is provided by the division's Watershed Condition Assessment (WCA) Program. The WCA Program partnered with the Pacific West Region to fund and oversee an assessment at each park in the Upper Columbia Basin Network (UCBN). This report documents the results of the Natural Resource Condition Assessment (NRCA) completed for Whitman Mission National Historic Site (WHMI).

Natural resource condition assessments are broad-scope ecological assessments intended to develop synthesis "information products" readily usable by park managers for: a) resource stewardship planning, and b) reporting to performance measures such as the DOI Strategic Plan's "land health" goals. Three elements are key to making these assessments useful for both planning and performance reporting:

1. Build on data, information, and knowledge already assembled through efforts of the NPS I&M Program, other NPS science support programs, and from partner collaborators working in and near parks;
2. Emphasize a strong geospatial component for how the assessment is conducted and in the resulting information products;
3. Provide narrative and/or semi-quantitative descriptions of science-based reference conditions for park resources that will assist parks as they work to define Desired Future Conditions through park planning processes. These reference conditions will become more refined and quantitative over time.

Information gained from this report will form the basis for development of actions to reduce and prevent impairment of park resources through park and partnership efforts. The goals of the natural resource condition assessment are to:

- Determine the state of knowledge concerning overall natural resource condition
- Identify information gaps and resource threats
- Assess overall ecosystem health
- Sets the stage to establish the context for management actions and collaboration

This report is designed to give park staff a moment-in-time assessment of the natural resources of Whitman Mission National Historic Site. This report will describe the natural resources of the park (both aquatic and upland), determine the state of knowledge on their condition using existing data or new data collected at priority sites for this project, identify information gaps, draw conclusions or hypotheses on the condition of natural resources (unknown, degraded, unimpaired), identify resource threats or potential issues affecting ecosystem health, and recommend further studies.

Study Area

Park Setting

WHMI was established in 1936 to preserve the 98.15 acre site (Figure 1) of a mission founded in 1836 by Marcus and Narcissa Whitman among the Cayuse Indian people of the Inland Pacific Northwest. The site was the first American settlement in the Pacific Northwest and became an important way station along the Oregon Trail. WHMI is located at the southern extreme of the Palouse Prairie region of southeastern Washington approximately 7 miles west of Walla Walla, Washington. The topography is generally flat with the elevation ranging from 615' to 724' at the top of Memorial Hill.

Resource management at this site is dedicated to preserving the archeological, historical and landscape values associated with the original Whitman Mission during the time from 1836 to 1847. These include native vegetation and landscape features that existed during the occupation of the mission.

The general management plan for WHMI has 2 major objectives (NPS 2000). The first is to protect and preserve the cultural and natural resources of the Whitman Mission. Strategies to achieve this objective include:

- Inventory cultural and natural resources.
- Manage, update, and maintain the park's resource information database (includes GIS).
- Manage and protect park collections and archives
- Manage and protect park structural landscape component, including monuments, graves, and landscape features.
- Implement and sustain a cultural and natural resource program.
- Implement a monitoring program.
- Use IPM/fire to protect park resources.

Whitman Mission National Historcial Site

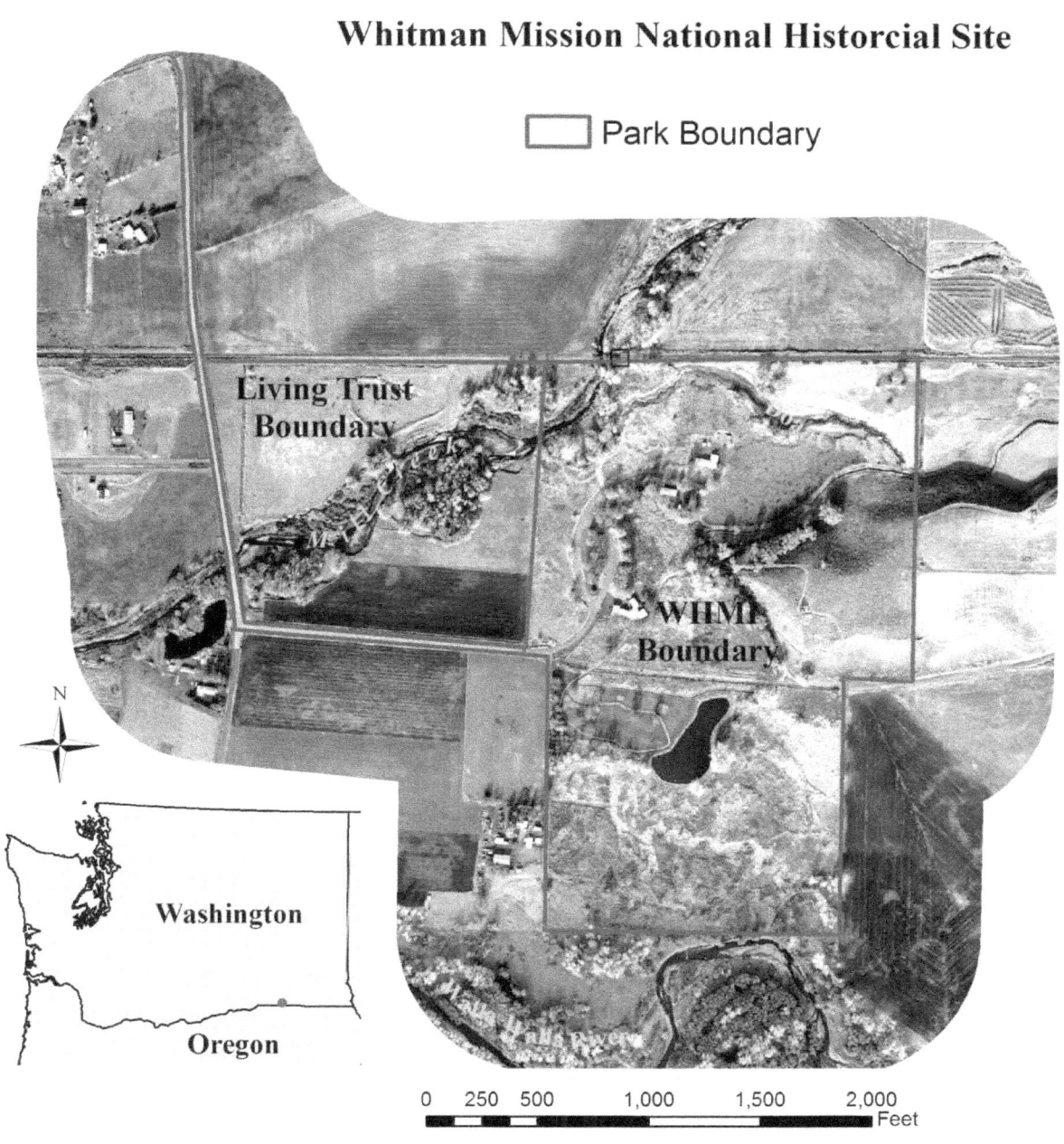

Figure 1. Map of WHMI park boundaries.

The second major objective listed in the general management plan is to restore and preserve the park's natural resources, including riparian and wetland areas, and the cultural landscape. Strategies listed to achieve this objective include:

- Identify options for Doan Creek and irrigation ditch management and implement the selected option.
- Manage vegetation.
- Collaborate with other federal and state agencies in the protection of hydrologic and aquatic resources.

WHMI visitation at the park reached a high of 151,800 visitor days in 1976 and has slowly been decreasing since to a recent low of 49,337 in 2007 (Figure 2). Visitor days/year has averaged 63,065 over the past 10 years. There is no over-night camping at WHMI so visitor use is limited to day use.

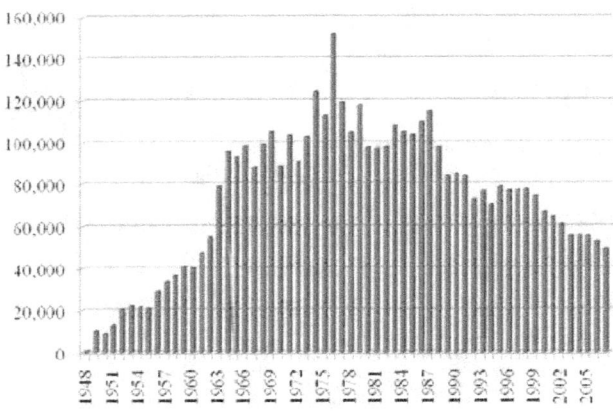

Figure 2. Visitor use days per year at WHMI from 1948-2007.

Historical Setting

The Cayuse people were the original inhabitants in the lands surrounding the WHMI. This land was called Wai-i-lat-pu, "Place of the People of the Rye Grass." The Cayuse practiced very little crop agriculture, depending instead on a partially nomadic existence that emphasized food gathering, raising livestock in the form of horses, and salmon fishing. Fire was used periodically by the Cayuse to burn particular areas to increase the production of wild forage and accessibility of plant foods, to facilitate hunting and travel. The regularity with which the areas on or near the historic site were burned historically cannot be determined, but frequent cultural burning of any particular area was probably rare.

WHMI was the first permanent Euro-American settlement in the Inland Northwest. In 1836, Dr. Marcus and Narcissa Whitman, along with the Reverend Henry and Eliza Spalding, were sent by the American Board of Commissioners for Foreign Missions to minister among the Indians in the Northwest. The Whitmans established the mission on a large triangle of flat, fertile land formed by the Walla Walla River and a tributary, Mill Creek. The Mission was occupied until 1847, when the Whitmans and 11 others were killed in an uprising by the Cayuse.

WHMI is managed as a historical park to preserve 5 major purposes.

1. Document and preserve the establishment of Whitman Mission and the subsequent massacre as important events in western pioneer history and settlement.
2. Tell the story of Whitman Mission as a clash between two cultures and their lack of understanding and ability to solve problems peacefully. One culture a white, American missionary society and the other, the native culture of the Cayuse
3. Preserve the site of Whitman Mission as an important component of the Oregon Trail. The Mission was one of seven aid stations along the trail and provided an important respite for emigrants during the early years of the Oregon Trail.
4. To document and memorialize the massacre of the Whitmans and eleven others, which lead to an unsuccessful end of the Mission and led to a war between the militia and the Cayuse in 1848.
5. Preserve the Mission Grounds, the site of the Great Grave, and the memorials to the Whitmans.

It is likely that the Cayuse used the resources at the site at least periodically for centuries before the mission was established. Archeological evidence of modification of natural conditions has not been documented. However, soon after the mission was established, an irrigation system was developed, crops were planted, and areas were opened to grazing by draft livestock and cattle. A considerable number of stock animals moved through the mission from the Oregon Trail, and there was ample opportunity for the introduction of exotic plants. The changes that occurred to the plants and landscape during the time the mission was extensive; the introduction of domestic livestock, exotic plants and agriculture, and the removal of riparian vegetation for fire and building wood.

Land Cover
WHMI is located on the southern extreme of the Palouse Prairie Region. Originally, perennial bunch grasses flourished in swards over the rolling prairie. Large native herbivores were generally absent from the Palouse, and because of this, the grasses evolved with a low resistance to grazing. Subsequent grazing by domestic livestock and extensive cultivation for wheat are the main reasons native perennial grasslands are now rare on the Palouse prairie.

It is probable that in 1836 at the time the mission was established, a mixture of three plant communities occupied the site (Romo and Krueger 1985). The Walla Walla River flowed through the site during times of high water. The floodplains along the Walla Walla River and nearby Mill Creek were dominated by a narrow plant community consisting of dense tangled thickets of willows (*Salix* spp.), black cottonwood (*Populus balsamifera ssp. trichocarpa*), red-osier dogwood (*Cornus stolonifera*), blackberries (*Rubus* spp.), elderberry (*Sambucus cerulea*), and other species common to riparian communities. Intermixed throughout the site was giant wild ryegrass (*Leymus cinereus*) a species preferring a year-round supply of soil moisture and occurring primarily on clay bottomlands and seepage areas. It now occurs as scattered large bunches of grass, but historically, it may have been more extensive and is the basis for the Cayuse name "Wai-i-lat-pu." Bluebunch wheatgrass (*Pseudoroegneria spicata*) and Sandberg's bluegrass (*Poa secunda*) dominated the higher elevation and drier sites.

WHMI has 190 plant specimens documented in their herbarium and currently there are no known federally listed threatened or endangered plant species, list available at website http://science.nature.nps.gov/im/units/ucbn/inventory/index.cfm#table.

Vegetation data was available from the LANDFIRE Program (USFS and USGS 2008). The vegetation map was created through a predictive modeling approach using a combination of field reference information, 2000 Landsat imagery, and spatially explicit biophysical gradient data. Map units are derived from National Vegetation Classification System (NVCS) Ecological Systems classification (Comer et.al. 2003). The data was clipped by the watershed boundaries (described in the following section "Watersheds"), then summarized by class (Table 1), and mapped (Figure 3) for the 68,271 acre WHMI watershed area.

Table 1. List of Ecological Systems with acres and percentage found in the WHMI project area.

NVCS Ecological Systems	Acres	Percentage
Agriculture-Cultivated Crops and Irrigated Agriculture	20,415	29.90%
Agriculture-Pasture/Hay	30,095	44.08%
Columbia Basin Palouse Prairie	291	0.43%
Columbia Plateau Steppe and Grassland	817	1.20%
Developed-High Intensity	191	0.28%
Developed-Low Intensity	5,299	7.76%
Developed-Medium Intensity	2,128	3.12%
Developed-Open Space	5,548	8.13%
Inter-Mountain Basins Big Sagebrush Shrubland	979	1.43%
Inter-Mountain Basins Big Sagebrush Steppe	559	0.82%
Inter-Mountain Basins Mixed Salt Desert Scrub	86	0.13%
Inter-Mountain Basins Montane Riparian Systems	748	1.10%
Introduced Upland Vegetation-Annual Grassland	500	0.73%
Northern Rocky Mountain Dry-Mesic Montane Mixed Conifer Forest	129	0.19%
Northern Rocky Mountain Ponderosa Pine Woodland and Savanna	167	0.25%
Rocky Mountain Montane Riparian Systems	317	0.46%

The land cover within the 3 watersheds of the WHMI project area is dominated by agriculture (73.98%). The project area has a significant developed land use type (11.16%) due mainly from the town of Walla Walla and the surrounding communities. There is 8.13% of the project area in rural development, 'Developed-Open Space.' The balance of land (6.93%) in the project area is classified as native and non-native dominated grass, shrub, and tree dominated vegetation, which is found mainly in the higher elevations of the watersheds.

Whitman Mission National Historic Site

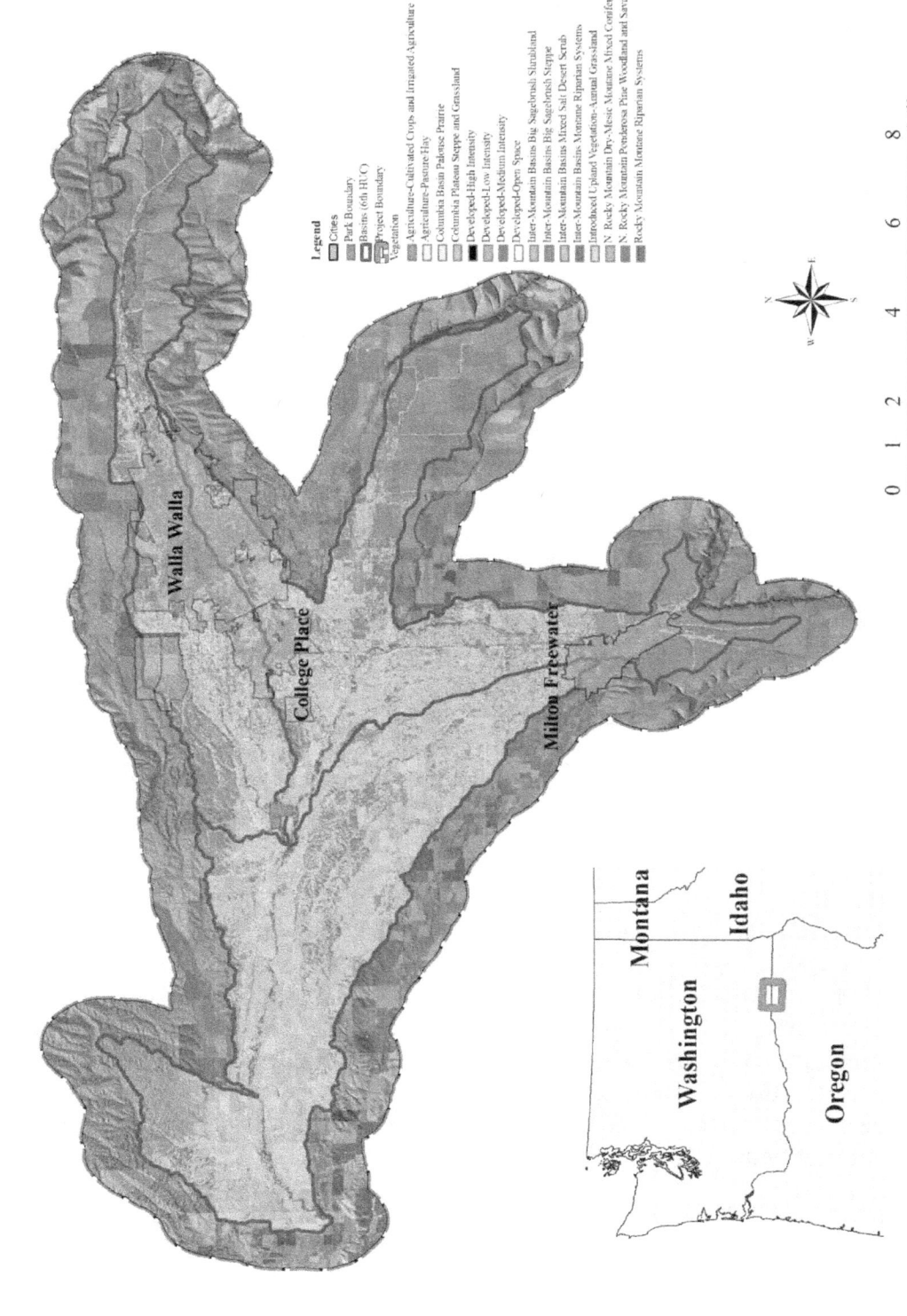

Figure 3. Map of vegetation types for the WHMI project area.

Upland Habitats/Species

Wildlife at WHMI is represented primarily by a variety of small rodents. Twenty-seven mammal species were confirmed during a 2003 inventory (Rodhouse et al. 2003). The most common mammals are cottontail rabbit (*Sylvilagus* spp.), voles (*Microtus* spp.), deer mice (*Peromyscus maniculatus*), western harvest mice (*Reithrodontomys microps*) and northern pocket gopher (*Thomomys talpoides*). Also present are feral house cats, which can be serious predators on small rodents and migratory passerine birds. Bird surveys documented 202 species at WHMI (Rodhouse et al. 2003). Of the 202 observed bird species 85 were unexpected and not previously documented at WHMI. There are no federally listed species known to use or occasionally pass through the WHMI. A complete list of mammal, bird, reptile, and amphibian species can be found on the UCBN website;
http://science.nature.nps.gov/im/units/ucbn/inventory/index.cfm#table.

A total of 3 amphibians and 5 reptiles were documented at WHMI during 2002 (Rodhouse et al. 2003). Bullfrogs are abundant around the Millpond, Mill Creek, and along the irrigation channel. Common garter snakes, gopher snakes and painted turtles have been observed at various locations throughout the site. The 2002-2003 inventories confirmed for the first time the occurrence of the great basin spadefoot (*Spea intermontana*) toad.

WHMI has non-native plants in all areas of the park. By 1985, a major emphasis in maintenance at the site was on revegetation and the control of non-native plant species (Gilbert 1984, Romo and Krueger 1985). Since that time, vegetation management has converted 60% of the site from exotic grasses and weeds to grasses that grew in the area during Whitman's era, or to grasses that have the same appearance as the native grasses. These native-appearing grasses will gradually be replaced with native species. In 1994, a vegetation plan was developed and implemented for Doan Creek and the surrounding area (NPS 2000). In 1997, NPS staff conducted an inventory of exotic plant species identified the following six species of concern: field bindweed (*Convolvulus arvensis*), jointed goatgrass (*Aegilops cylindrica*), poison hemlock (*Conium maculatum*), yellow starthistle (*Centaurea solstitialis*), Canada thistle (*Cirsus Canadensis*), and Scotch thistle (*Onopordum acanthium*) (NPS 2000).

Watersheds

River and stream drainages are uniquely identified by hydrologic unit codes (HUC). These are geographic areas based on surface topography containing a major river or a group of smaller rivers identified by 2 digits representing each level, for a total of 12 digits to describe the lowest level (HUC6). The Pacific Northwest is number 17 of the 21 regions (HUC1) in the United States. The second level divides the 21 regions into 222 subregions. Subregions are areas drained by a river system, a reach of a river and its tributaries, a closed basin, or a group of streams forming a coastal drainage area. The third level subdivides the subregions into 352 basins and at HUC4 there are 2,149 drainages, referred to as subbasins.

WHMI is located in the Walla Walla River subbasin (HUC4 – 17070102), which drains an area of 1,758 square miles. WHMI lies near the intersection of 3 – 5th level HUCs; Middle Walla Walla River (1707010207), Mill Creek-Walla Walla River (1707010202), and Lower Walla Walla River (1707010211). Figure 4 is a map of the 3 – 6th level HUC's that form the project area for WHMI; Lower Mill Creek (170701020204), Garrison Creek-Walla Walla River (170701020704), and Mud Creek-Walla Walla River (170701021102).

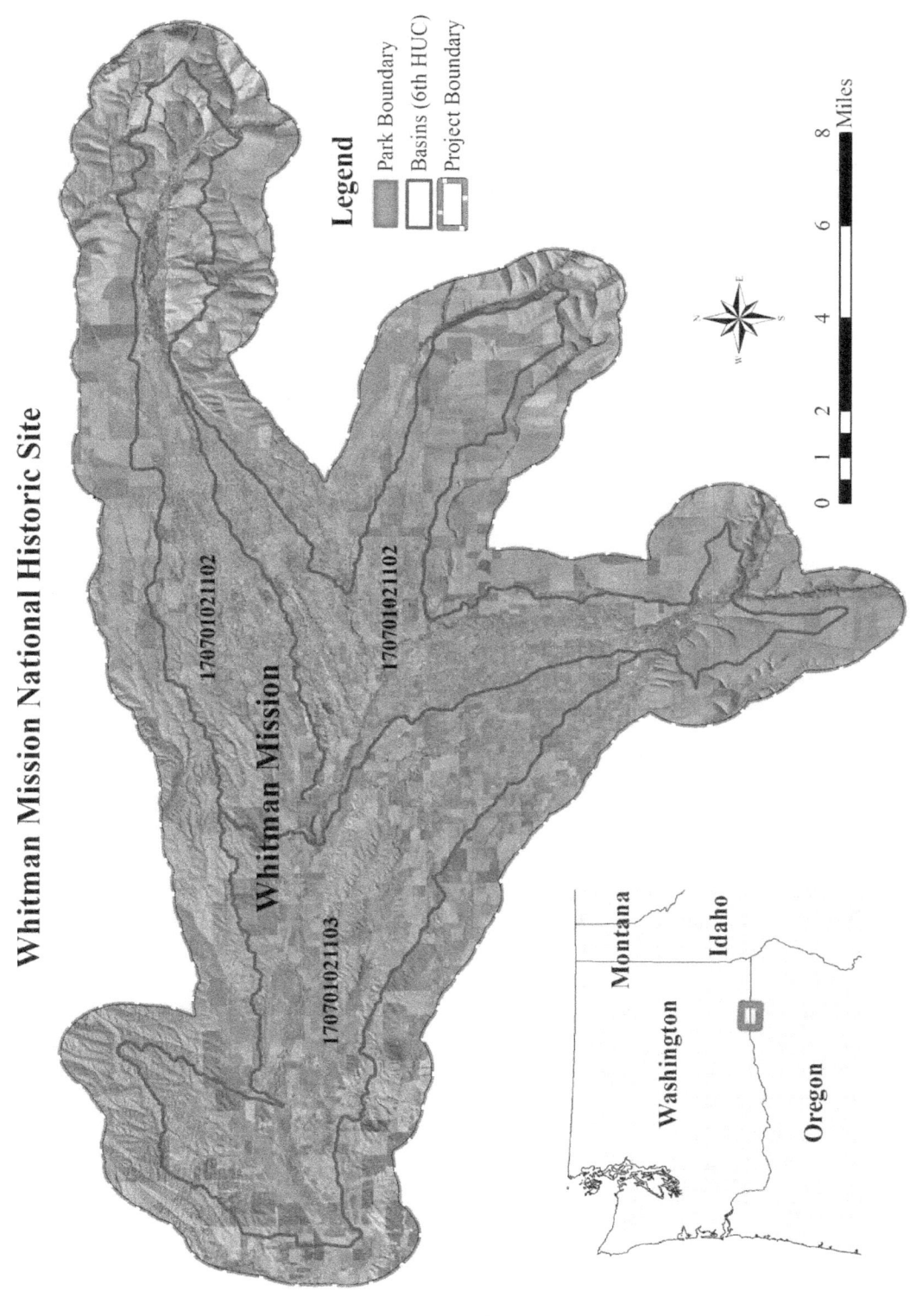

Figure 4. Map of the 6th level HUCs forming the project area for WHMI.

Aquatic Habitats/Species

Approximately ten acres of the WHMI is wetland, but not formally classified as such in any documents published by NPS, U.S. Army Corps of Engineers, National Wetlands Inventory, or Natural Resource Conservation Service. While there are no springs within WHMI, there are distinct former stream channels of Doan Creek and the Walla Walla River, which hold water in winter and spring. There is a wetland enhancement project planned by WHMI staff to unchannel Doan Creek along the northern boundary to allow more water to meander, creating more wetland habitat. The U.S. Army Corps of Engineers purchased land that borders the south boundary of the NHS and the north bank of the Walla Walla River. The State Department of Fish and Wildlife is administering this land as riparian habitat.

Surface water resources at WHMI include Mill Creek, Doan Creek, the Millpond, and an irrigation ditch. Mill Creek originates on the western slopes of the Blue Mountains, in southeastern Washington, at an elevation of 5,500 feet (USACE 1995). It flows for 15 miles in a relatively deep and narrow canyon, through mountainous terrain, and then enters an alluvial fan a few miles east of the City of Walla Walla. Mill Creek flows through the northern corner of the WHMI property where it collects streamflow from Doan Creek then enters the Walla Walla River about ½ mile west of WHMI.

Doan Creek is a left bank, spring-fed tributary of Mill Creek. Doan Creek originates three miles east of the WHMI and passes through a private airport, a former dairy, and agricultural land before entering the site at the northeastern boundary. From there, Doan Creek runs through a restored channel continuing west along the northern boundary until joining with Mill Creek. An irrigation water pumping station draws water out of Doan Creek into the irrigation ditch that supplies water to the park and to two downstream irrigators.

Washington Department of Fish and Wildlife (WDFW) has documented habitat for rainbow/steelhead trout (*Oncorhynchus mykiss*), speckled dace (*Rhinichthys osculus*), redside shiner (*Richardsonius balteatus*), 3 species of sculpins (*Cottus* spp.), and common carp (*Cyprinus carpio*) in Doan Creek (NPS 2003). WDFW also anticipates that the restored habitat on the WHMI property can support Chinook salmon *Oncorhynchus tshawytscha* and coho salmon *Oncorhynchus kisutch*.

The historic Millpond covers about two and one-half acres and is held by earthen dikes. The Millpond was restored in 1961, and is located on the eastern end of the mission grounds. The irrigation channel from Doan Creek supplies the Millpond with water. Marcus Whitman is credited with establishing the first irrigation ditch in this area. At least one irrigation ditch has crossed the mission grounds since Whitman's time. Currently, WHMI is responsible for maintaining 5,967 feet of irrigation ditch in accordance with Washington State law. The current irrigation ditch provides water for two farms to the west.

Climate

For the past 50 years the annual precipitation at Walla Walla Airport averages 19.34"/yr with 17.2" of snow during the winter months . The daily temperature varies as much as 40 degrees during the summer (Western Regional Climate Center, 2003). Mean monthly minimum/maximum temperatures ranges from 27.8°/39.5° F in January to 60.4°/89.2° F in July. Prevailing winds year around come from the southwest. Figure 5 and 6 shows the distribution of precipitation and average annual temperature zones within the WHMI project area, respectively.

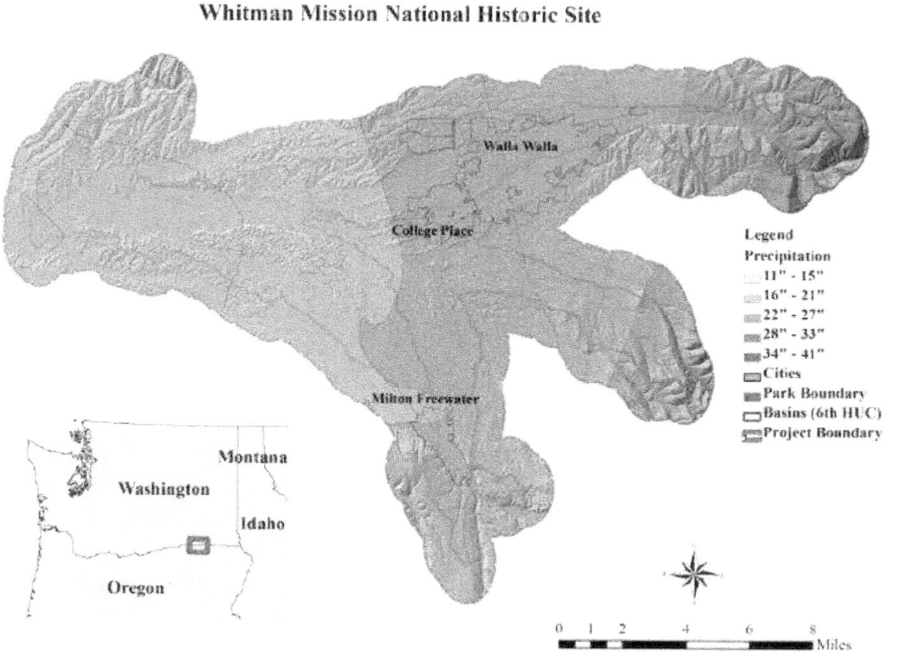

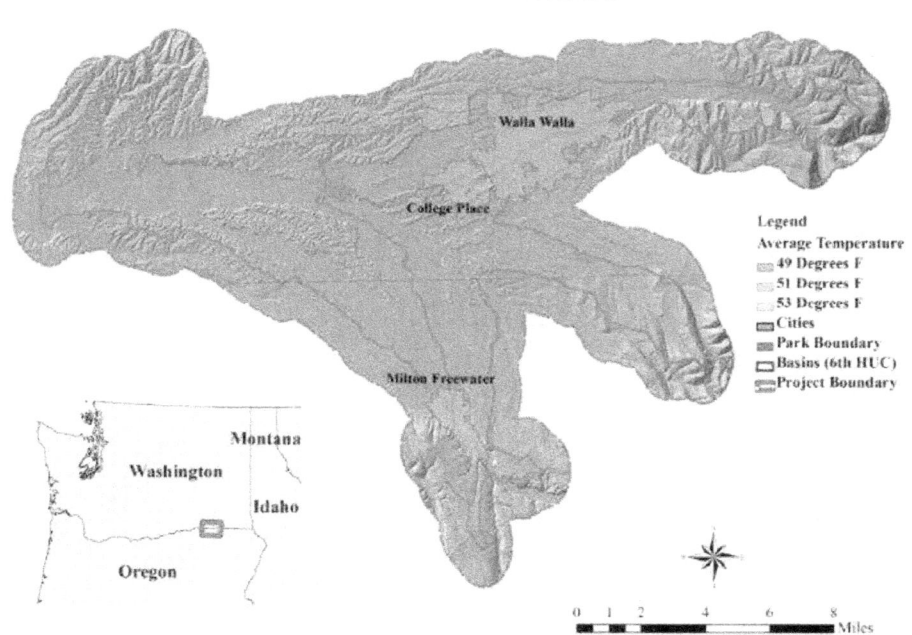

Figure 5. Map of precipitation zones in the WHMI project area

Figure 6. Map of average annual temperature zones in the WHMI project area.

Methods

GIS and Geodatabases

The majority of data used in this report is Geographical Information System (GIS) data in tabular form tied to spatial features, such as points, lines, and/or polygons. GIS software provides spatial analysis capabilities such as overlay, buffer, extraction, and modeling. Results can then be displayed in map and tabular form. GIS software ARCMap Version 9.3 was used to store, edit, and display data.

A map project file was developed for WHMI using ArcMap software that followed the behavioral rules for data in a single Microsoft Access database (Figure 7). Many types of geographic datasets can be collected within a map project file, including feature classes, attribute tables, and raster data sets. The NPS ArcMap 8½ "x11" template was used in the WHMI map project file.

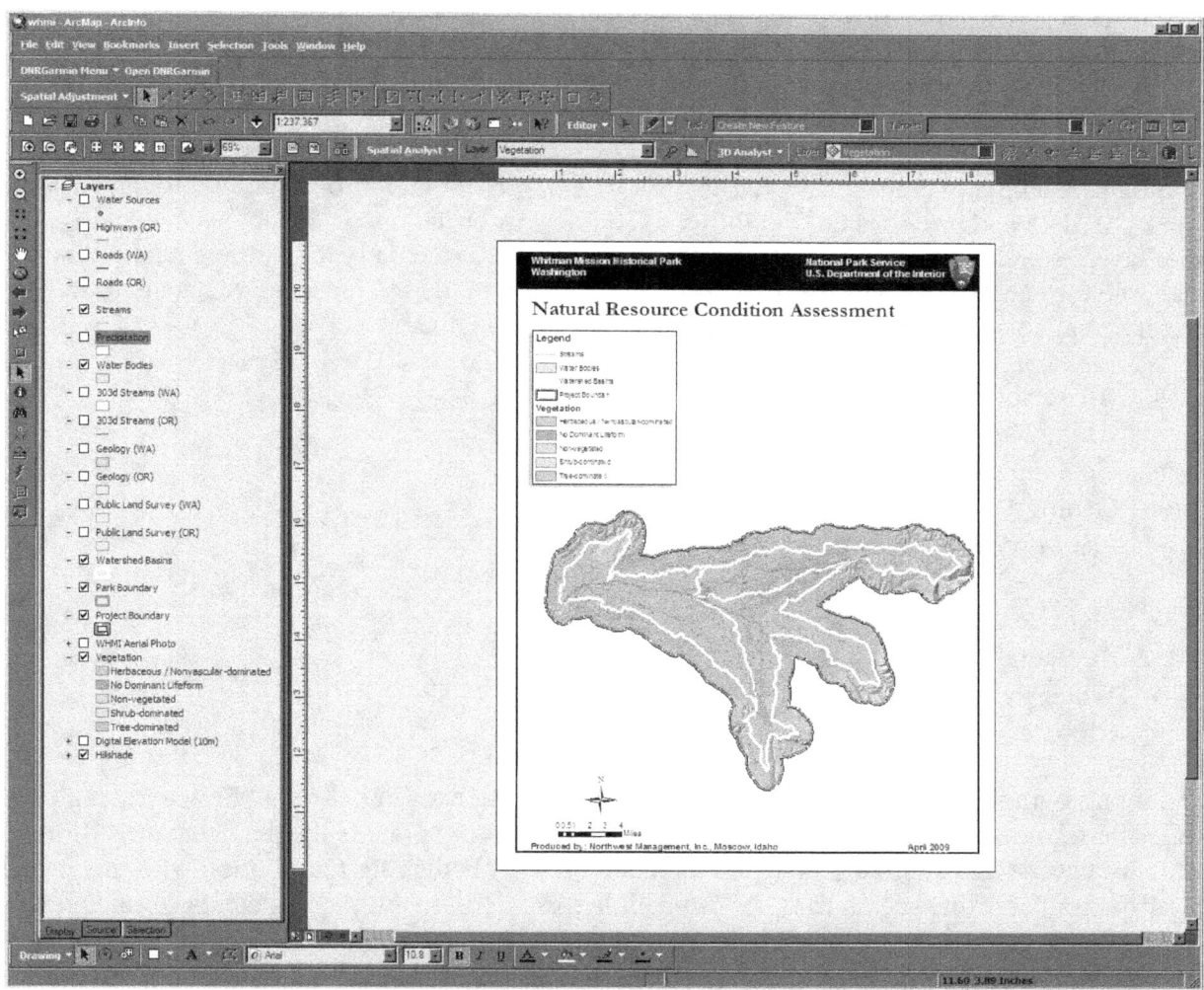

Figure 7. Screen capture of the ArcMap Project file for the WHMI project area.

A geographically defined project area was created by selecting 6th level HUC watersheds surrounding WHMI. A 2 kilometer buffer was added for mapping purposes (140,344 ac). General base map layers and aerial photography were developed to the full project area extent. Most layers were clipped to the watershed basin extent for analysis and summarization of attributes (68,653 ac).

The map project file was populated with GIS data through an extensive search of NPS sources and a multitude of local, state, and federal web sites. Data determined to be useful and accurate were re-projected into the North American Datum 1983 (NAD83) and the Universal Transverse Mercator (UTM) zone 11 projection. Metadata was generated for each layer in Federal Geographic Data Committee (FGDC) compliant format. Metadata describes the source, accuracy, data dictionary, projection, datum, and many other details about an individual layer. Aerial photography was processed and clipped to the project area using LizardTech GeoExpress software and converted into a MG3 (MrSid Generation 3) format file.

Attribute information on the specific data layers clipped to the watershed basin extent were summarized in a spreadsheet based on the various attribute parts, lengths, acreage, etc. of the various data layers in the map project file.

All GIS data layers were imported into an ArcGIS File Geodatabase using ArcCatalog ver. 9.3 (ESRI 2006). Feature data sets were created based on theme type. A geodatabase is an ArcMap file structure that stores geometry, spatial reference system, attribute datasets, network datasets, topologies, and many other features. This GIS format provides a uniform method for storing and using GIS data and provides the flexibility to add new information as it becomes available. Map layers were organized into categories based on general theme type. Although data was not available for each theme type, the category directory is included to incorporate data that may become available in the future. The general themes used include:

- Air Resources
- Animal
- Geography
- Geology
- Land Process
- Land Use
- Plant
- Stressors
- Water Resources
- Climate

Aerial photography was not included in the geodatabase due to limitation in the processing of MG3 file formats. Aerials are included in a separate directory outside the geodatabase. All the data, project file and summary table are included on a DVD disk for distribution with this report. As a by-product of the search for GIS compatible data, a Microsoft Access database (included on DVD) was created for websites with documented GIS data that could be downloaded in various formats and is compatible with ESRI's ArcMap software. The database has a custom query form for doing searches on the 3,000+ entries that cover 3 states; Oregon, Washington, and Idaho.

NPS Data Sources

Additional non-GIS data was acquired from searches on the internet, such as NPS NatureBib (https://science1.nature.nps.gov/naturebib), and from direct contact with local and state government agencies. WHMI is in the Upper Columbia Basin Network (UCBN) established under the NPS Inventory and Monitoring Program (NPS 1999). Table 2 is the status of inventories of the species taxa groups for WHMI. Available data from completed inventories were utilized where needed in the report otherwise, the data is directly available at the UCBN website http://science.nature.nps.gov/im/units/ucbn/inventory/index.cfm#table. Invasive plant species inventories, a subset of vascular plant inventories, are in progress, however no inventories are available for fish, invertebrates, or rare plants.

Table 2. Status of inventories of species taxa for WHMI maintained by the UCBN.

Species Taxa	Complete	Year Completed	In Progress	Not Complete
Mammals	✓	2003		
Birds	✓	2003		
Amphibians	✓	2003		
Reptiles	✓	2003		
Fish				✓
Invertebrates				✓
Vascular Plants	✓	unknown		
Rare Plants				✓
Invasive Plants			✓	

Additional non-biological data sets have been identified by the UCBN as important for park management (Table 3). Both the biologic and non-biologic inventories were considered as baseline information for development of the UCBN vital signs monitoring plan (Garrett et al. 2007). Three data sets have not been completed by the UCBN however some park sites may have data available from other sources.

Table 3. Status of inventories of non-biological data for WHMI maintained by the UCBN.

Non-Biologic Data sets	Complete	Year Completed	In Progress	Not Complete
Air Quality/Emissions				✓
Ozone Risk	✓	2001		
Water Quality	✓	1997		
Landcover				✓
Paleo Resources	✓	2005		
Geology	✓	2008		
Soils				✓
Cultural Landscapes				✓

The UCBN Monitoring Plan (Garrett et al. 2007) identifies a suite of 14 vital signs chosen for monitoring implementation in the UCBN parks over the next 5 years. Vital signs are "a subset of physical, chemical, and biological elements and processes of park ecosystems that are selected to represent the overall health or condition of park resources with known or hypothesized effects of stressors, or elements that have important human values" (NPS-UCBN http://science.nature.nps.gov/im/monitor/). Not all vital signs are monitored at each park. WHMI has 7 vital signs established for monitoring; stream/river channel characteristics, surface water dynamics, water chemistry, aquatic macroinvertebrates, invasive/exotic plants, riparian vegetation, and land cover and use (Garrett et al. 2007).

Noxious Weeds

Noxious weeds of importance to WHMI were identified in Garrett et al. 2007. A complete list of Washington's noxious weeds can be found at http://www.nwcb.wa.gov/weed_list/weed_list.htm. They are classified into 3 categories based on control requirements; Class A (eradicate), Class B (contain) and Class C (control). GIS data on noxious weeds was extracted from a geodatabase developed by the UCBN for management of the parks integrated pest management (IPM). The geodatabase was maintained for 4 years from 2002-2005. Summary statistics by species and maps were developed from the data. State and county level databases were searched for noxious weed locations and the Walla Walla County weed superintendent was contacted for unpublished data. Available data have been summarized on maps and tables in the Results section.

Upland Assessment

Vegetation Restoration Management Units (VRM) for WHMI were first developed by Gilbert (1984), later refined by Romo and Krueger (1985), then documented by Garrett and Coyner (2003). The VRM units are the basic management unit for WHMI staff and are used for the site specific assessment. The assessment method was co-developed by the Natural Resources Conservation Service (NRCS), Agricultural Research Service (ARS), Bureau of Land Management (BLM), and the United States Geological Survey (USGS). The method is described in the publication "Interpreting Indicators of Rangeland Health" (Pellant et al., 2005).

Site specific data was collected on August 15, 2008. A complete list of plant species was not attempted due to the time of year. Plant species identification followed the species list found at the UCBN website, http://science.nature.nps.gov/im/units/ucbn/inventory/index.cfm#table. Appendix C is a complete list of all species identified at each plot with percent canopy cover.

The rangeland health rapid assessment methodology was designed to provide a preliminary evaluation of 3 landscape attributes; soil/site stability, hydrologic function, and integrity of the biotic community at the ecological site level. It was developed to assist land managers in identifying areas that are potentially at risk of degradation and assist in the selection of sites for developing monitoring programs. Definitions of these three closely interrelated attributes are:

> *Soil Site Stability:* The capacity of the site to limit redistribution and loss of soil resources (including nutrients and organic matter) by wind and water.
> *Hydrologic Function*: The capacity of the site to capture, store, and safely release water from rainfall, run-on (inflow), and snowmelt (where relevant), to resist a reduction in this capacity, and to recover this capacity following degradation.
> *Integrity of the Biotic Community*: The capacity of the site to support characteristic functional and structural communities in the context of normal variability, to resist loss of this function and structure due to disturbance, and to recover following disturbance.

This technique was developed as a tool for conducting a moment-in-time qualitative assessment of rangeland status and as a communication and training tool for assisting land managers and other interested people to better understand rangeland ecological processes and their relationship to indicators (Pyke at. el. 2002) This method uses soil survey information, ecological site descriptions, and appropriate ecological reference areas to qualitatively assess rangeland health. As part of the assessment process, 17 indicators relating to these attributes are evaluated and the category descriptor or narrative that most closely describes the site is recorded. "Optional Indicators" may also be developed to meet local needs. The critical link between observations of indicators and determining the degree of departure from the ecological site description and/or ecological reference area is part of the interpretation process.

This technique does not provide for just one rating of rangeland health, but is based upon a "preponderance of evidence" qualitative approach. It rates each site in the departure from the ecological site description/ecological reference area(s) for the three attributes: soil site stability, hydrologic function, and biologic integrity. There are 5 categories of departure recognized, "none to slight," "slight to moderate," "moderate," "moderate to extreme," and "extreme."

A slight modification of the methodology was implemented because the park has been under a revegetation program since 1985 and all areas of the park have been heavily utilized for farm or grazing in the past as documented in Garrett and Coyner (2003). The objective of the WHMI general management plan (NPS 2000) is to maintain the visual aspect of the historic period at the time the Whitman Mission was active. The plan calls for revegetation using both native and non-native species along with noxious weed management. Past land management practices have left WHMI in various states of recovery. The evaluation of indicators 10, 12, 13, 14, 15, and 17 were based on the desired vegetation identified for each VRM in Gilbert (1984).

Indicators were converted to a numerical rating to allow calculating a percent departure value. A rating from 1 (none to slight) to 5 (extreme) was assigned to the 5 evaluation categories. There are 10 indicators for soil site stability and hydrologic function and 9 for biotic integrity. The score for each landscape attribute was the sum of the indicators minus the reference conditions; which was determined to be 10 for soil site stability and hydrologic function and 9 for biotic integrity based on a score of 1 for each indicator per attribute. Percent departure for each attribute was a proportion calculated by dividing the score by the maximum departure value,(40 for soil stability and hydrologic function and 35 for biotic integrity) and expressed as a percentage. The results are displayed graphically as a percent departure from the reference condition. For the narrative the percent departure values are converted back into the associated qualitative categories: none to slight (<20%), slight to moderate (20-39%), moderate (40-59%), moderate to extreme (60-79%), and extreme (≥80%).

A Microsoft Access database was developed for digitally storing site data, comments, and the 17 indicator values. A GPS point was collected at the center of each sample site along with 4 digital pictures taken facing the cardinal directions. Sample sites varied from 1 to 20 acres in size as noted in the database. Maps were generated for each VRM depicting evaluation sites and other land features. The point data was also placed in the geodatabase for future reference.

Aquatic Assessments

Evaluation of onsite aquatic resources at WHMI included an assessment of the riparian resource condition of Doan Creek and Mill Creek and an assessment of the in-stream condition of Mill Creek based upon benthic macroinvertebrate indicators. Benthic macroinvertebrates were not collected from Doan Creek due to the lack of stream flow during the onsite evaluation.

Riparian Habitat

Riparian habitat serves many functions, including erosion control, stream shading and cooling, providing woody debris, insect production, and stream bank stabilization. Riparian areas often contain the greatest resource diversity and productivity in the watershed (Barber 2005). Riparian areas serve as a buffer between aquatic habitat (e.g., streams and rivers) and upland activities. In addition, these areas often contain wetlands where water is filtered, retained, and slowly released to the river throughout the year.

Mill Creek and Doan Creek were assessed using the "proper functioning condition" (PFC) riparian assessment method developed by the Bureau of Land Management (Prichard et al. 1998). The PFC method evaluates 17 hydrology, vegetation, and stream geomorphology indicators of riparian condition or "health" and subsequently assigns a functionality rating to each site.

The "proper functioning condition" of a riparian area refers to the stability of the physical system, which in turn is dictated by the interaction of geology, soil, water, and vegetation. A properly functioning riparian area is in dynamic equilibrium with its streamflow forces and channel processes. The channel adjusts in slope and form to handle larger runoff events with limited perturbation of channel characteristics and associated riparian/wetland plant communities. Because of this stability, properly functioning riparian areas can maintain fish and wildlife habitat, water quality enhancement, and other important ecosystem functions even after larger storms. In contrast, nonfunctional systems subjected to the same storms might exhibit excessive erosion and sediment loading, loss of fish habitat, loss of associated wetland habitat, and so on.

Based on assessments of the hydrologic, vegetative, and geomorphology elements of the riparian area, one of the following three functionality ratings is assigned to each site:

Proper Functioning Condition (PFC): Streams and associated riparian areas are functioning properly when adequate vegetation, landform, or large woody debris is present to:

1. Dissipate stream energy associated with high waterflows, thereby reducing erosion and improving water quality.
2. Filter sediment, capture bedload, and aid floodplain development.
3. Improve floodwater retention and groundwater recharge.
4. Develop root masses that stabilize stream banks against cutting action.
5. Develop diverse ponding and channel characteristics to provide habitat and the water depths, durations, temperature regimes, and substrates necessary for fish production, waterfowl breeding, and other uses.
6. Support greater biodiversity.

Functional - At Risk: These riparian areas are in functional condition, but an existing soil, water, vegetation, or related attribute makes them susceptible to degradation. For example, a stream reach may exhibit attributes of a properly functioning riparian system, but it may be poised to suffer severe erosion during a large storm in the future due to likely migration of a headcut or increased runoff associated with recent urbanization in the watershed. When this rating is assigned to a stream reach, its "trend" toward or away from PFC is assessed.

Nonfunctional: These are riparian areas that clearly are not providing adequate vegetation, landform, or large woody debris to dissipate stream energy associated with high flows, and thus are not reducing erosion, improving water quality, sustaining desirable channel and riparian habitat characteristics, and so on as described in the PFC definition. The absence of certain physical attributes such as a floodplain where one should exist is an indicator of nonfunctioning conditions.

PFC assessment does not refer to the successional stage of the riparian - wetland vegetation community (Biggam et al. 2005). Rather, the evaluation is based on the concept that in order to manage for such things as potential natural vegetation communities or desired fish and wildlife habitat features, the basic elements of physical stability (e.g., energy dissipation and streambank stabilization) must first be in place and functioning properly. For example, a vegetation community recovering from a recent fire may be in an early successional stage due to loss of trees and shrubs, but that stage may still provide sufficient physical stability for the riparian area to accommodate flood flows without significant erosion and channel change. That geomorphically stable and "properly functioning" condition allows for recovery of the desired features of later successional systems such as in-channel woody debris that creates desired fish habitat or riparian tree and shrub layers that provide diverse bird habitats.

During this site visit, the team assessed riparian functional condition on reaches of Mill Creek and Doan Creek within WHMI. The stream reach assessments are discussed individually below, and each assessment is supported by a detailed PFC assessment checklist in Appendix A.

Benthic Macroinvertebrates
Benthic macroinvertebrates (BMI) are well suited for biomonitoring assessments within rocky-substrate stream habitats for several reasons (Morley 2000; Fore et al. 1996):

1. The macroinvertebrate community is extremely diverse, represented by thousands of different species with a variety of feeding strategies.
2. The pollution tolerance levels of macroinvertebrates range from very high to very low.
3. Sampling macroinvertebrates can be performed with relative ease by a single individual with simple equipment.
4. The aquatic life spans of macroinvertebrates range from several weeks to several years, which provides an indication of stream quality over a period of time, not just the sampling window.
5. Unlike fish, macroinvertebrates are fairly limited in mobility, meaning they cannot avoid polluted areas. The adults will lay the eggs where they may and the benthic larvae are dependent upon the water quality and habitat to survive.
6. The methods for collecting, subsampling, preserving, and identifying macroinvertebrates are well established, facilitating comparison of data between sites.

7. Macroinvertebrates can be found in any aquatic habitat as long as the water quality is high enough to sustain them.
8. Macroinvertebrate communities can recover rapidly from repeated sampling events, providing the ability for repeated sampling.

Channel characteristics were observed and BMI samples were collected in the Mill Creek stream reach flowing through the northwest corner of the Whitman Mission property on May 14, 2008. A Surber sampler was used to collect three replicate BMI samples in a single, uniform riffle habitat unit within the creek. A Surber sampler was selected to collect BMI because it allows sampling a uniform 1-square-foot (144 square inch) area. Sampling began in the downstream portion of the riffle and proceeded upstream for the three replicates. At each replicate sampling location the following methodology was used:

1. Place Surber sampler on the selected sampling spot with the opening of the nylon net facing upstream. Brace the frame and hold it firmly on the creek bottom.
2. Lift the larger rocks resting within the frame and brush off crawling or attached loosely organisms so that they drift into the net.
3. Once the larger rocks are removed, disturb the substrate vigorously with a trowel or small rake for 60 seconds. This disturbance should extend to a depth of about 10 cm to loosen organisms in the interstitial spaces, washing them into the net.
4. Lift Surber out of the water. Tilt the net up and out of the water while keeping the open end upstream. This helps to wash the organisms into the receptacle.
5. On the creek bank, empty contents of Surber into large bucket. Rinse Surber and empty into bucket until all animals are removed. Great care should be taken in this step to collect and preserve all organisms from the Surber sampler as well as from the rocks and water in the bucket. Use of a magnifying glass and tweezers is essential. Rinse bucket through sieve to remove water from sample. Pick out large debris (sticks and leaves) after carefully removing any invertebrates.
6. Use spatula to move sample from sieve into a plastic vial. Fill vial to the top with isopropyl alcohol. Put label on inside of vial with name of sampler, date, and location. Write location and date on top of vial lid.
7. Return to the location of the first sample, walk upstream and collect another sample of invertebrates. Repeat this process once more for a total of three replicate samples from each site location. The three replicates are combined into one composite sample for shipment to the laboratory for analysis.

All BMI samples were shipped to ABR, Incorporated in Forest Grove, Oregon for sorting, identification, and analysis. Each sample was processed using standard laboratory sample handling and labeling protocols. A Caton gridded tray was used to subsample 500 organisms from original samples. Using this subsampling procedure, each sample was evenly distributed across a 30-square wire-mesh tray. Individual squares were randomly selected and the contents removed and placed into a Petri dish. Macroinvertebrates were removed from the sample material under a dissecting microscope. This process was repeated until 525-550 organisms were subsampled. The remainder of the sample (the unsorted fraction) was then inspected for large or rare taxa that were not encountered during the subsampling procedure; these "large/rare" taxa were recorded on the laboratory bench sheet as such and placed in a separate vial. The following products resulted from the sample sorting procedure:

1. 525-550 macroinvertebrates sorted into a series (4-7) of small vials by order, class, and/or phylum.
2. A separate vial containing organisms found during the large-rare search (if performed).
3. Sorted residue material from which the 525-550 organisms were sorted.
4. Unsorted fraction portion of the original sample that was not sorted.

Macroinvertebrate identification also followed standard protocols. Macroinvertebrates were identified to the lowest practical taxonomic level, generally genus or species for most taxonomic groups, excepting mites, Oligochaetes, microcrustaceans, and *Chironomidae*.

All raw data were entered into Excel spreadsheets and were crosschecked against paper copies of the data for errors and omissions before the data were analyzed. Data were analyzed with a multimetric index known as the Benthic Index of Biotic Integrity or B-IBI. The B-IBI utilizes information concerning the abundance and composition of a stream's benthic macroinvertebrate community to assess the overall biological integrity of the stream ecosystem. As such, "biological integrity" is defined as "the ability to support and maintain a balanced, integrated, adaptive community of organisms having a species composition, diversity and functional organization comparable to that of natural habitat of the region" (Karr and Dudley 1981). In practice, the B-IBI provides quantitative scores for 10 metrics that describe individual key attributes of the benthic macroinvertebrate community. Scores for the 10 metrics are summed and the cumulative site score is categorized into a level of impairment based on a predetermined scale.

Since macroinvertebrate communities differ from region to region, multimetric indexes have been developed and calibrated for use within particular regions or states. Currently, no multimetric tools are available for use with eastern Washington macroinvertebrate data (Hayslip 2007), including data from the Mill Creek site. However, multimetric tools are available for use in the neighboring regions of northeastern Oregon (OR IBI) and Idaho (Idaho Stream Macroinvertebrate Index, or SMI). These tools were used to analyze the Mill Creek data to provide a basis for comparison of potential future samples collected at the Mill Creek site. It should be noted that Mill Creek occurs in the Columbia Plateau Level III ecoregion, which overlaps into northeastern Oregon and portions of northern Idaho suggesting that the use of the Oregon IBI and Idaho SMI in analyzing eastern WA macroinvertebrate samples is not unrealistic. The Mill Creek site results are presented without suggesting that one of the two analysis tools is more appropriate than the other. Categorical scales established for the Idaho SMI and the eastern Oregon IBI are detailed below (Table 4 and 5).

Table 4. Eastern Oregon Index of Biotic Integrity (IBI) Impairment Categories.

Rating	Index Score Range
No Impairment	>41
Moderate Impairment	35-41
High Impairment	27-34
Severe Impairment	<27

Table 5. Idaho Stream Macroinvertebrate Index (SMI) Impairment Categories

Rating	Northern Mountains	Central and Southern Mountains	Basins
		Index Score Range	
Very Good	84-100	800-100	76-100
Good	65-83	59-79	51-75
Fair	44-64	40-58	34-50
Poor	22-43	20-39	17-33
Very Poor	0-21	0-19	0-16

Results

GIS and Geodatabase

The WHMI Geodatabase was populated with 23 shapefiles and images (Appendix A). These are all accessible from the ArcGIS Map Project file located on the DVD included with this report. Additional copies are available from the Upper Columbia Basin Network's website http://science.nature.nps.gov/im/units/ucbn/reports/.

Upland Site Specific Assessments

This section is an evaluation of each VRM unit. Figure 8 is a map showing the location of the original 5 – VRM units described by Gilbert (1984) and Figure 9 is a map of the current 18 VRM units. Table 6 summarizes the acres and percentage of the original and current VRM units.

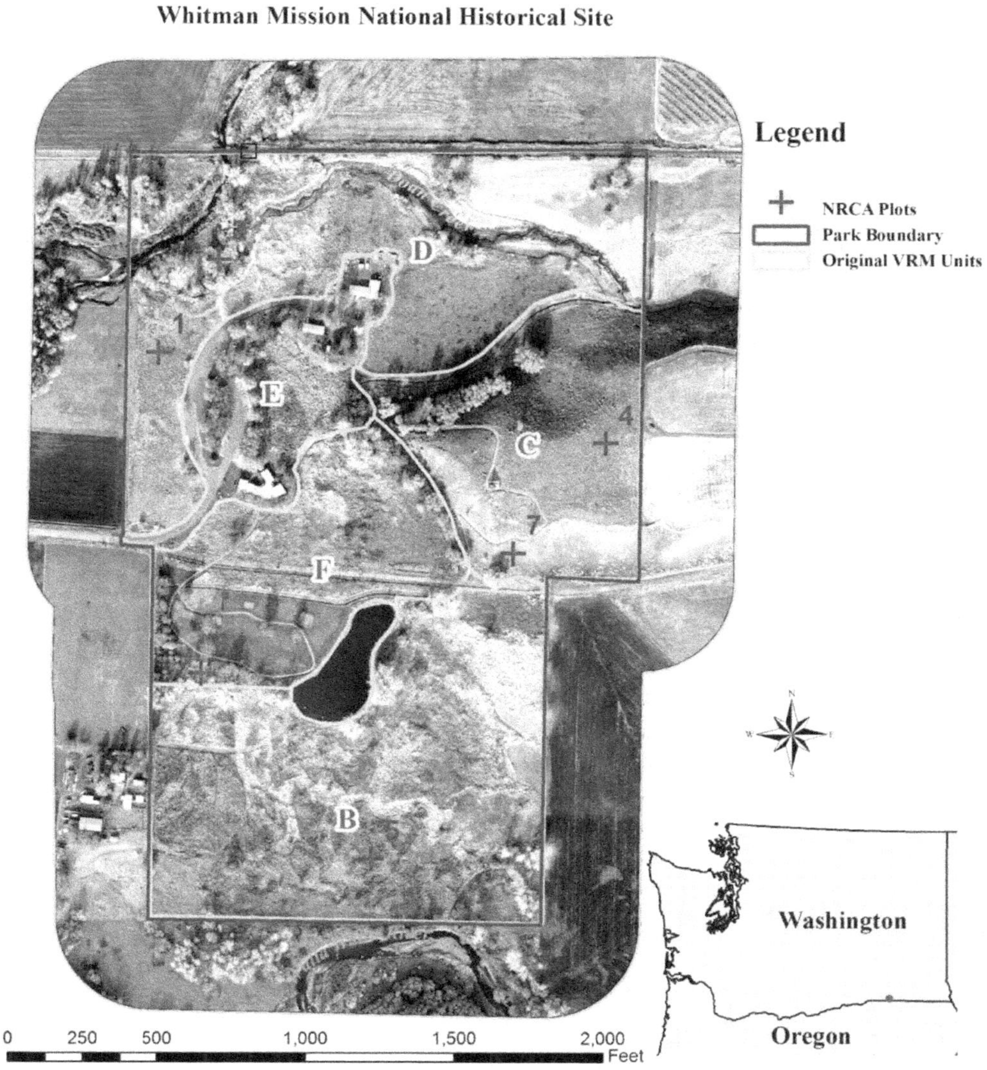

Figure 8. Map of the original VRM units in WHMI.

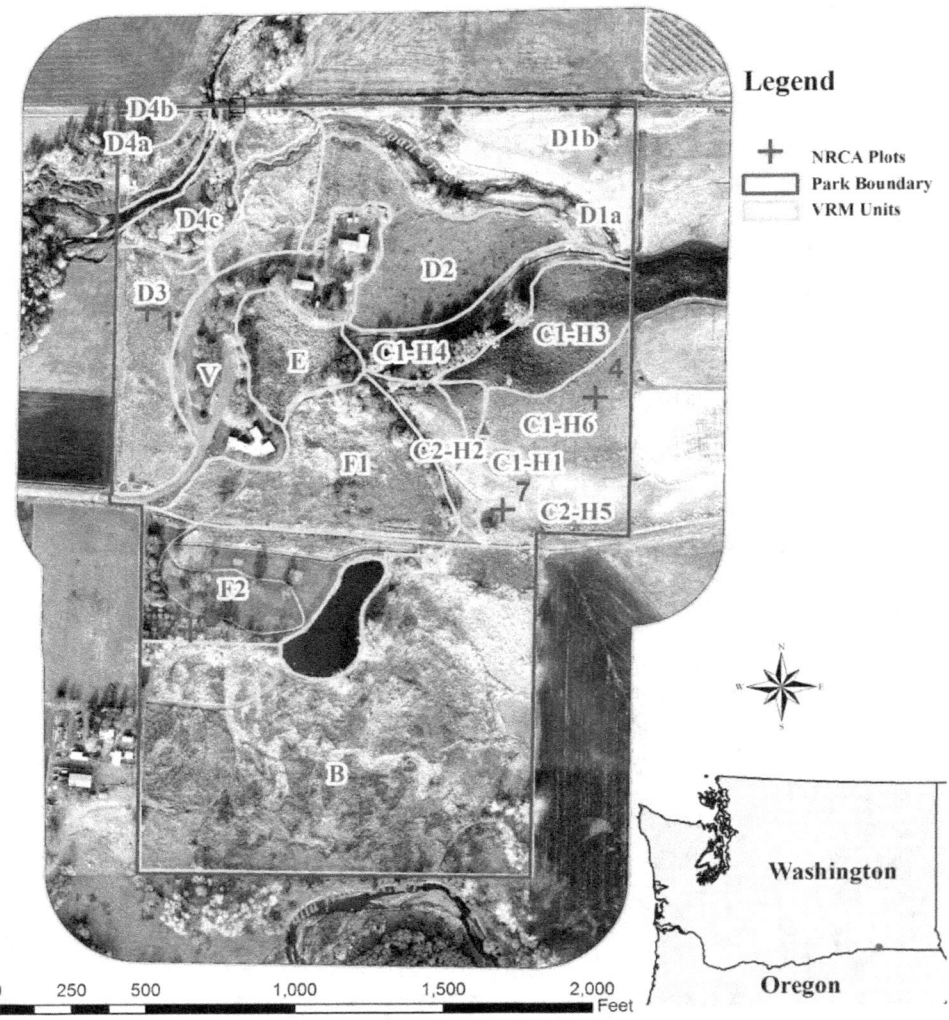

Figure 9. Map of current VRM units in WHMI.

Table 6. Summary of acres and percent of total area for the current and original VRM units in WHMI.

VRM Units	Unit (ac)	Unit (%)	Original VRM Units	Unit (ac)	Unit (%)
B	27.68	29.32%	B	27.68	29.32%
C1-H1	0.89	0.95%			
C1-H3	3.71	3.93%			
C1-H4	2.89	3.07%			
C1-H6	3.58	3.79%			
C2-H2	1.94	2.06%			
C2-H5	1.98	2.10%			
			C	15.03	15.92%
D1a	5.50	5.83%			
D1b	2.84	3.00%			
D2	7.12	7.54%			
D3	7.82	8.28%			
D4a	1.28	1.35%			
D4b	0.57	0.60%			
D4c	2.13	2.25%			
			D	26.69	28.27%
E	2.62	2.78%	E	9.19	9.73%
F1	7.68	8.13%			
F2	6.38	6.76%			
			F	14.07	14.90%
Monument	0.03	0.03%			
Mill Pond	1.75	1.85%	Mill Pond	1.75	1.85%
Mill Creek	0.47	0.50%			
V	5.56	5.89%			

Ecological sites are the basic land unit used in the assessment method documented in Pellant (2005) and are defined by soil type. For rangeland soils, ecological reference sites have been developed by the NRCS across the United States and in Washington they are available online at http://efotg.nrcs.usda.gov/treemenuFS.aspx. There are 9 soil types in WHMI representing 6 ecological sites (Figure 10). Table 7 summarizes the area and percentage of each soil type and ecological site. Pedigo silt loam is the most abundant soil type (49.39%) and the ecological sites Alkali Loamy 15+ PZ (R009XY401WA) and Alkali Loamy 9-15 PZ (R008XY401WA) are the most common ecological sites at 49.39% and 17.4%, respectively.

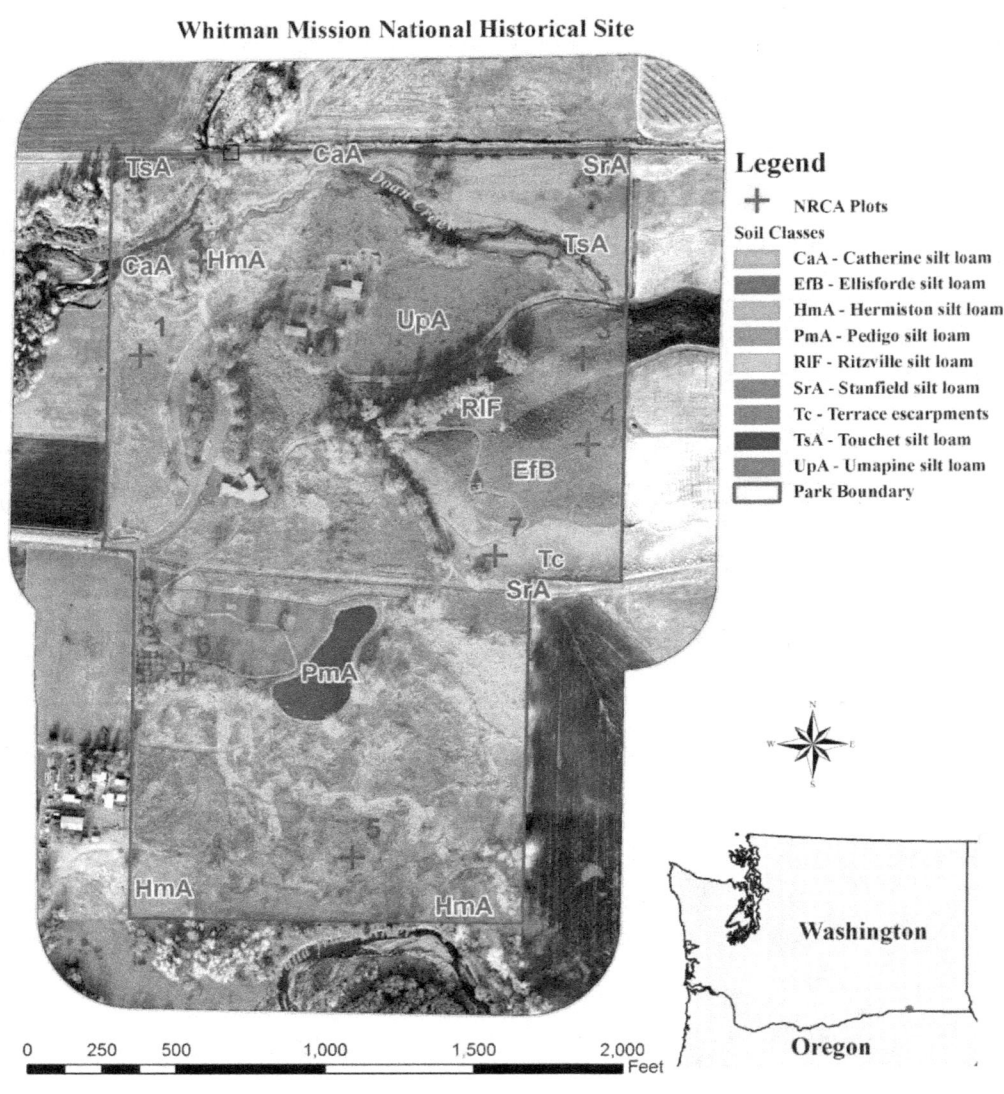

Figure 10. Map of soil types at WHMI.

Table 7. Summary of soil types and ecological reference sites at WHMI.

Soil Map Symbol	Soil Name	Acres	Percent	Ecological Reference Sheet No.	Ecological Reference Sheet Name	Plot No.
CaA	Catherine silt loam	2.83	2.98%	R008XY601 WA	Wet Meadow 9-15 PZ	2
EfB	Ellisforde silt loam	5.76	6.07%	R008XY102 WA	Loamy 9-15 PZ	4
HmA	Hermiston silt loam	8.79	9.26%	RO08XY401 WA	Alkali Bottom 9-15 PZ	
PmA	Pedigo silt loam	46.87	49.39%	R009XY401 WA	Alkali Bottom 15+ PZ	5, 6
RlF	Ritzville silt loam	2.75	2.90%	R008XY103 WA	Cool Loamy 9-15 PZ	3
SrA	Stanfield silt loam	0.40	0.42%	R008XY401WA	Alkali Bottom 15+ PZ	
Tc	Terrace escarpments	3.24	3.41%	R008XY103 WA	Cool Loamy 9-15 PZ	7
TsA	Touchet silt loam	7.33	7.72%	RO08XY401 WA	Alkali Bottom 9-15 PZ	
UpA	Umapine silt loam	16.93	17.84%	R007XY701WA	Alkali Bottom 6-9 PZ	1

VRM – B

VRM – B is approximately 27.7 acres (29.32%) located in the south 1/3 of WHMI (Figure 11). The unit has historically been used as pasture for livestock grazing, mainly cattle. Since 1986, grazing has been restricted in this unit to implement a revegetation plan. Garrett and Coyner (2003) documented the extensive work completed to plant, burn, spray, and plant the unit to control weeds and create a historically acceptable landscape. The unit is mainly a Pedigo silt loam soil that is classified as an Alkali Bottom 15+PZ (R009XY401WA) ecological reference site. Based on the ecological reference site, the historical climax plant community is wild rye (*Leymus cinereus*) – bluebunch wheatgrass and falls in the Columbia Basin Palouse Prairie Ecological System (NatureServe 2009).

One plot was evaluated in the unit (Figure 12). The soil stability and hydrologic function attributes were rated as none-slight departure (5.0% and 12.5%, respectively). The biotic integrity attribute was rated moderate (45.7%) due to the presence of invasive plants and the poor condition of perennial plants . The old oxbows of the Walla Walla River were dominated by reed canarygrass (*Phalaris aurundenacia*), which provides excellent soil stability but poor habitat for other riparian and native species.

The unit is in relatively good condition for soil and hydrologic function and not a threat for soil erosion. The biotic function is in better condition than documented in 1984 and 1985 (Gilbert 1984, Romo and Krueger 1985). There is excessive build up of litter that may be due in part to poor functioning of soil microorganisms. Excessive straw buildup is also frequently seen in dryland crop management when converting to a direct seed tillage operation. In these cases, burning is generally not recommended as a method for dealing with excessive straw and litter (STEEP 2008). Research has found that straw decomposes faster when in contact or near the soil. Mowing or rolling in late fall may be the most effective method to facilitate the decomposition of the past years' growth and incorporate it into the soil (STEEP 2008). Over time soil fungi and bacteria levels will increase and improve decomposition rates, which may reduce the need for mowing in the future.

Figure 11. Map of VRM-B and NRCA plot 5 in WHMI.

Figure 12. Departure from reference condition of the 3 landscape attributes in the Alkali Bottom 15+PZ ecological site at VRM-B, WHMI (background is of plot 5).

28

VRM – C1-H3

VRM – C1-H3 is approximately 3.71 acres (3.93%) of WHMI located on the north side of Memorial Shaft Hill (Figure 13). The unit was historically used as a pasture for livestock grazing, mainly cattle. Records indicate the unit has had no recent grazing and in 1986 a revegetation plan was implemented (Gilbert 1984). Garrett and Coyner (2003) documented the extensive work completed to plant, burn, spray, and plant the unit to control weeds and create a historically acceptable landscape. The unit is mainly a Ritzville silt loam soil that is classified as a Cool Loamy 9-15PZ (R008XY103WA) ecological reference site. Based on the ecological reference site, the historical climax plant community is Idaho fescue (*Festuca idahoensis*) - bluebunch wheatgrass and falls in the Columbia Basin Palouse Prairie Ecological System (NatureServe 2009).

One plot was evaluated in the unit (Figure 14). The soil stability and hydrologic function attributes were rated as none-slight departure (12.5% and 17.5%, respectively). The biotic integrity attribute was rated slight-moderate (31.4%) due to the presence of invasive plants. The site is dominated by cheatgrass (*Bromus tectorum*) and yellow starthistle (*Centaurea solstitialis*), but there are a few native species, such as snow buckwheat (*Eriogonum niveum*), growing in the unit. This unit has enough litter and vegetation to protect against soil erosion.

The unit is in relatively good condition for soil and hydrologic function and not a threat for soil erosion. The biotic function is in better condition than documented in 1984 and 1985 (Gilbert 1984, Romo and Krueger 1985). However, there is still a very high dominance of yellow starthistle. Continued treatment with herbicide spot spraying will reduce the vigor and health of the yellow starthistle while improving the ability of native forbs to establish viable populations. The hot dry summers experienced at WHMI reduce the competitiveness of native species over already established non-native and noxious species. WHMI's staff has a record of working with researchers in weed control and revegetation techniques. Recommendations are to continue this cooperation, to find non-native species that can compete with current noxious weeds, and meet the objective of restoring a historically acceptable landscape. WHMI staff should continue to seek noxious weed control techniques that are species specific such as biological control.

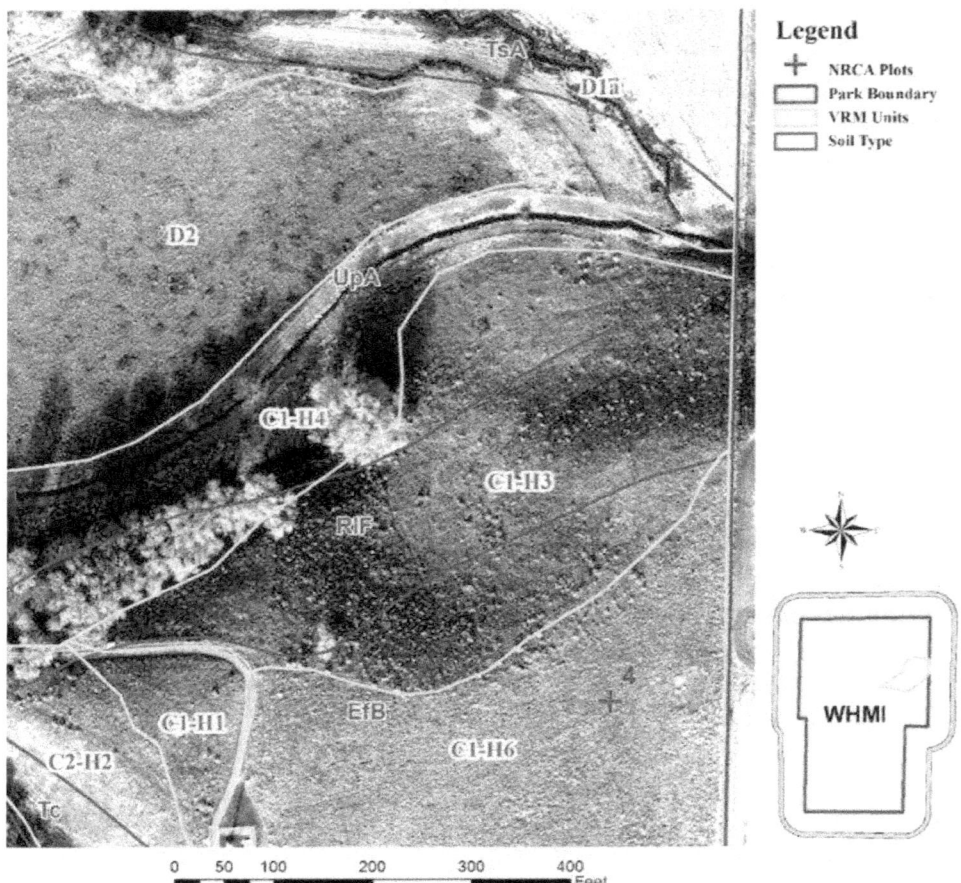

Figure 13. Map of VRM-C1-H3 in WHMI.

Figure 14. Departure from reference condition of the 3 landscape attributes in the Cool Loamy 9-15PZ ecological site at VRM-C1-H3, WHMI (background is of plot 3).

VRM – C1-H6

VRM – C1-H6 is approximately 3.58 acres (3.79%) of WHMI located on the top of Memorial Shaft Hill and is very similar to VRM – C1-H1, which is 0.89 acres (0.95%) and lies directly to the west (Figure 15). The unit was historically used as a pasture for livestock grazing, mainly cattle, and as a crop field. Records indicate the unit has had no recent grazing or farming and in 1986 a revegetation plan was implemented (Gilbert 1984). Garrett and Coyner (2003) documented the extensive work completed to plant, burn, spray, and plant the unit to control weeds and create a historically acceptable landscape. The unit is mainly an Ellisforde silt loam soil that is classified as a Loamy 9-15PZ (R008XY102WA) ecological reference site. Based on the ecological reference site, the historical climax plant community is bluebunch wheatgrass – Sandberg's bluegrass and falls in the Columbia Basin Palouse Prairie Ecological System (NatureServe 2009).

One plot was evaluated in the unit (Figure 16). All 3 landscape attributes; soil stability, hydrologic function, and biotic integrity; were rated none-slight departure (5.0%, 5.0%, and 11.4%, respectively). The site is dominated by bluebunch wheatgrass and bluegrass (*Poa sp.*) with very few noxious weeds. The site was planted in 1991 and has been a very successful. There were few native forb species detected in the unit, which is due to the noxious weed control program. The unit has enough litter and vegetation to protect against soil erosion and is close to meeting the reference condition for the ecological site.

The biotic function is in better condition than documented in 1984 and 1985 (Gilbert 1984, Romo and Krueger 1985). WHMI staff have recognized the lack of native forb species and in 2000 changed their noxious weed control program to spot spray with herbicides (Garrett and Coyner 2003). The staff also introduced 2 biological control agents for yellow starthistle stands on the adjacent hillsides to reduce reproduction capabilities. Even with the hot dry summers experienced at WHMI, this unit is proof that under the right conditions a competitive stand of native species can be established and maintained. WHMI's staff has a record of working with researchers in weed control and revegetation techniques. Recommendations are to continue this cooperation to find noxious weed control techniques that are species specific such as biological control.

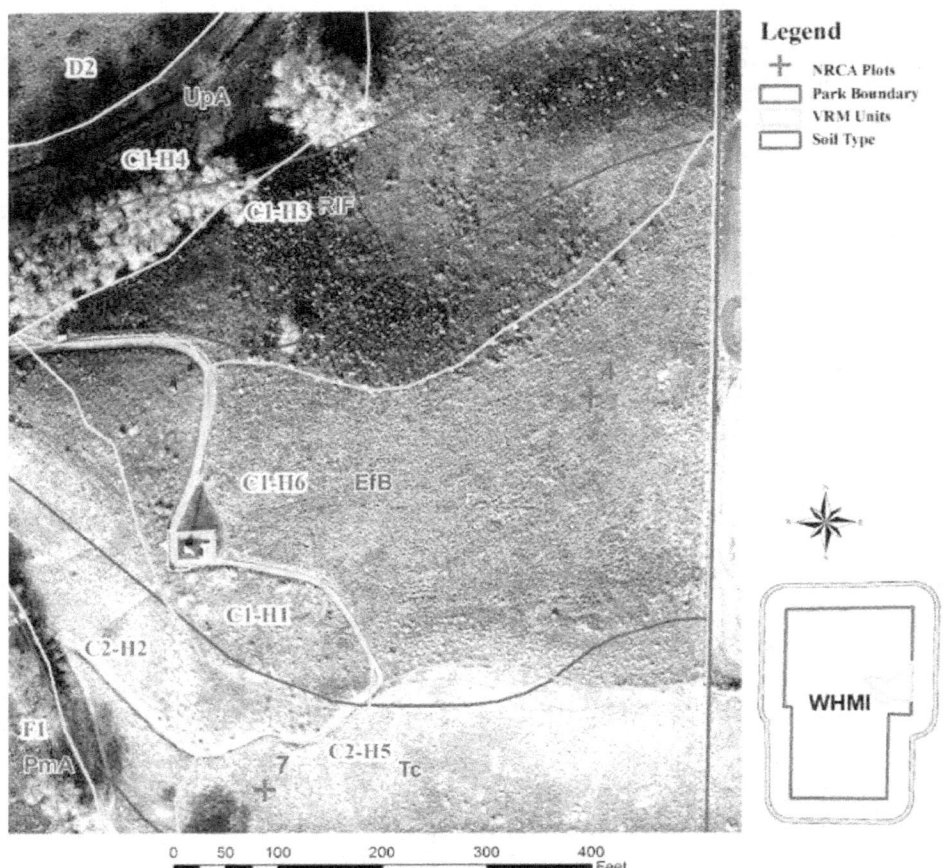

Figure 15. Map of VRM-C1-H6 in WHMI.

Figure 16. Departure from reference condition of the 3 landscape attributes in the Loamy 9-15PZ ecological site at VRM-C1-H6, WHMI (background is of plot 4).

VRM – C2-H5

VRM – C2-H5 is approximately 1.98 acres (2.1%) of WHMI located on the south side of Memorial Shaft Hill and is very similar to VRM – C2-H2, which is 1.94 acres (2.06%) and lies directly to the northwest (Figure 17). The unit was historically used as a pasture for livestock grazing, mainly cattle. Records indicate the unit has had no recent grazing and in 1986 a revegetation plan was implemented (Gilbert 1984). Garrett and Coyner (2003) documented the extensive work completed to plant, burn, spray, and plant the unit to control weeds and create a historically acceptable landscape. The unit is classified as a Terrace escarpment, which did not have an ecological site description. Examination of the Walla Walla County soil map revealed similar conditions just to the east being classified as an Ellisforde silt loam (15-30% slope). This soil type was used for assessment of the ecological site, which is classified as a Loamy 9-15PZ (R008XY102WA). Based on the ecological reference site, the historical climax plant community is bluebunch wheatgrass/Sandberg's bluegrass and falls in the Columbia Basin Palouse Prairie Ecological System (NatureServe 2009).

One plot was evaluated in the unit (Figure 18). The soil stability and hydrologic function attributes were rated as none-slight departure (7.5% and 17.5%, respectively). The biotic integrity attribute was rated moderate (45.7%) due to the presence of invasive plants and the lack of perennial species. The site is dominated by cheatgrass (*Bromus tectorum*) (80% canopy cover) and yellow starthistle (*Centaurea solstitialis*) (10% canopy cover), but there are a few native species, such as snow buckwheat (*Eriogonum niveum*), growing in the unit. The unit has enough litter and vegetation to protect against soil erosion, especially compared to a reference condition.

These units are in relatively good condition for soil and hydrologic function and not a threat for soil erosion even though it has the steepest slopes in WHMI. The biotic function is in similar condition as documented in 1984 and 1985 (Gilbert 1984, Romo and Krueger 1985). Even with the planting effort following Romo and Krueger (1985) after a wildfire in 1998, the species composition has changed little. There is still a dominance of cheatgrass and yellow starthistle in the unit. Continued treatment with herbicide spot spraying will reduce the vigor and health of the yellow starthistle while improving the ability of native forbs to maintain or increase their populations. The hot dry summers experienced at WHMI reduce the competitiveness of native species over many of the already established non-native and noxious species. Solutions to the revegetation effort will require additional efforts following specialist's recommendations. WHMI's staff has a record of working with researchers in weed control and revegetation techniques. Recommendations are to continue this cooperation to find non-native species that can compete with current noxious weeds and meet the historical landscape objective. WHMI staff should continue to use noxious weed control techniques that are species specific such as biological control.

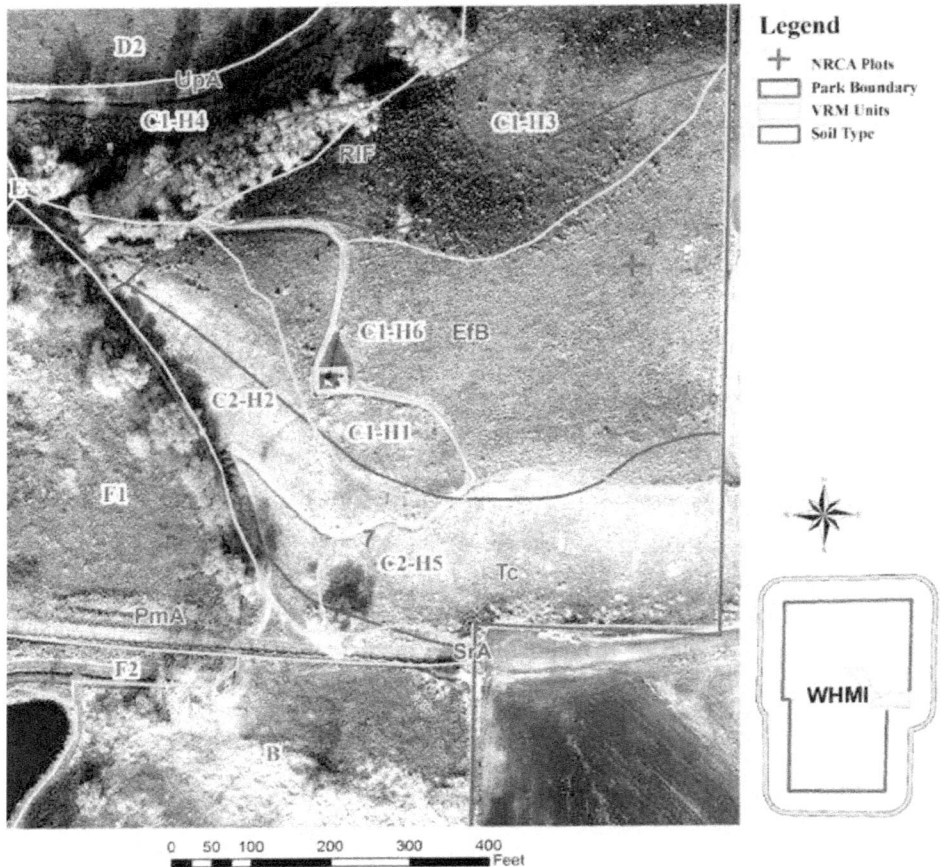

Figure 17. Map of VRM-C2-H5 in WHMI.

Figure 18. Departure from reference condition of the 3 landscape attributes in the Loamy 9-15PZ ecological site at VRM-C2-H5, WHMI (background is of plot 7).

VRM – D3

VRM – D3 is approximately 7.28 acres (8.28%) of WHMI located west of the visitor's center bordering the west boundary (Figure 19). The unit was historically used as cropland. Records indicate the area has no recent grazing or farming and in 1986 a revegetation plan was implemented (Gilbert 1984). Garrett and Coyner (2003) documented the extensive work completed to plant, burn, spray, and plant the unit to control weeds and create a historically acceptable landscape. The unit has 3 soil types; Hermiston silt loam (4.10 acres), Pedigo silt loam (2.27 acres), and Umapine silt loam (1.35 acres). The Hermiston silt loam was used for analysis and is classified as an Alkali Bottom 9-15PZ (R008XY401WA) ecological reference site. Based on the ecological reference site, the historical climax plant community is basin wildrye/bluebunch wheatgrass and falls in the Columbia Basin Palouse Prairie Ecological System (NatureServe 2009).

One plot was evaluated in the unit (Figure 19). All 3 landscape attributes; soil stability, hydrologic function, and biotic integrity; were rated none-slight departure (12.5%, 15.0%, and 14.3%, respectively). The site is dominated by tall wheatgrass (*Thinopyrum ponticum*) with few noxious weeds. The site was planted in 1990 and was successfully revegetated. There were few native forb species detected in the unit, which is due to the noxious weed control program and the lack of available native species. The unit was cropland for many years, which removed all native species. The unit has more litter and vegetation than predicted in the ecological reference site. This provides protection against soil erosion, but is creating problems for decomposition of the past years' biomass. This is also reflected in the very high rating for soil surface resistance to erosion due to the lack of any soil structure in the A or B soil horizons.

All the landscape attribute functions are in better condition than documented in 1984 and 1985 (Gilbert 1984, Romo and Krueger 1985). WHMI staff have recognized the lack of native forb species and use spot spraying in their noxious weed control program (Garrett and Coyner 2003). WHMI staff recognize the problem with litter buildup and have used prescribed fire several times in the past to reinvigorate the stand (Garrett and Coyner 2003). Burning can have a negative impact on soil organic material when repeated too often. The excessive build up of litter may be due in part to the poor functioning of soil microorganisms. Excessive straw buildup is also frequently seen in dryland crop management when converting to a direct seed tillage operation. In these cases, burning is generally not recommended as a method for dealing with excessive straw and litter (STEEP 2008). Research has found that straw decomposes faster when in contact or near the soil. Mowing or rolling in late fall may be the most effective method to facilitate the decomposition of the past years growth and incorporate it into the soil (STEEP 2008). Over time soil fungi and bacteria levels will increase and improve decomposition rates, which may reduce the need for mowing in the future.

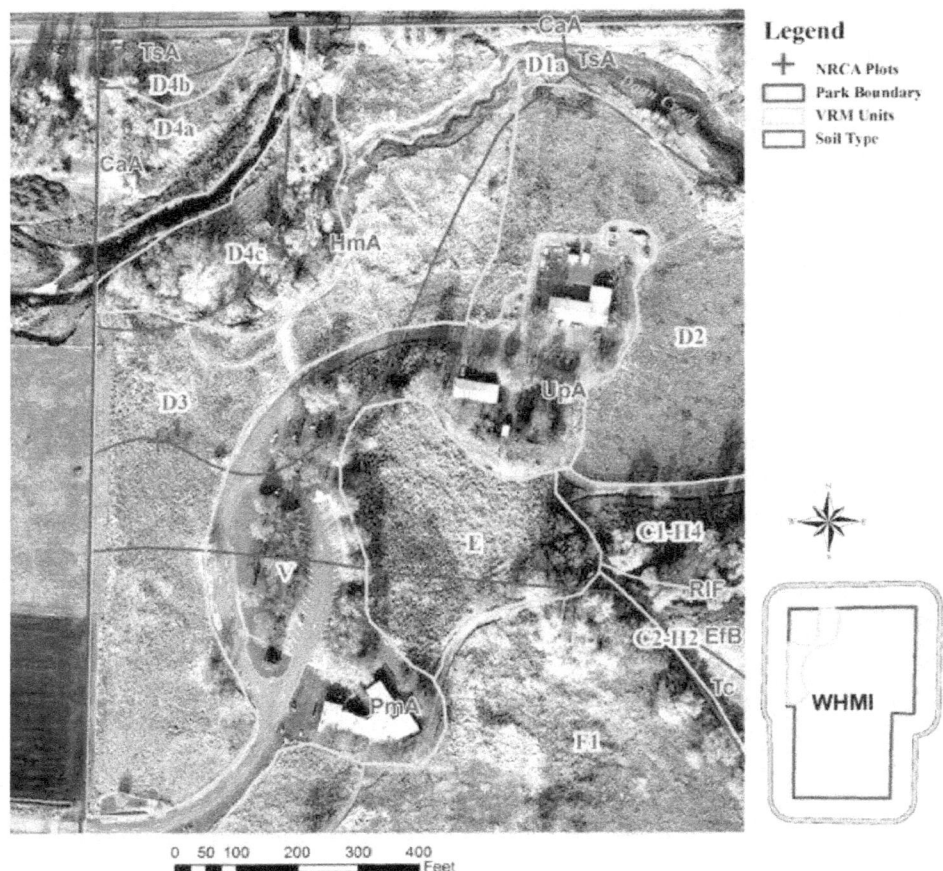

Figure 19. Map of VRM – D3 in WHMI.

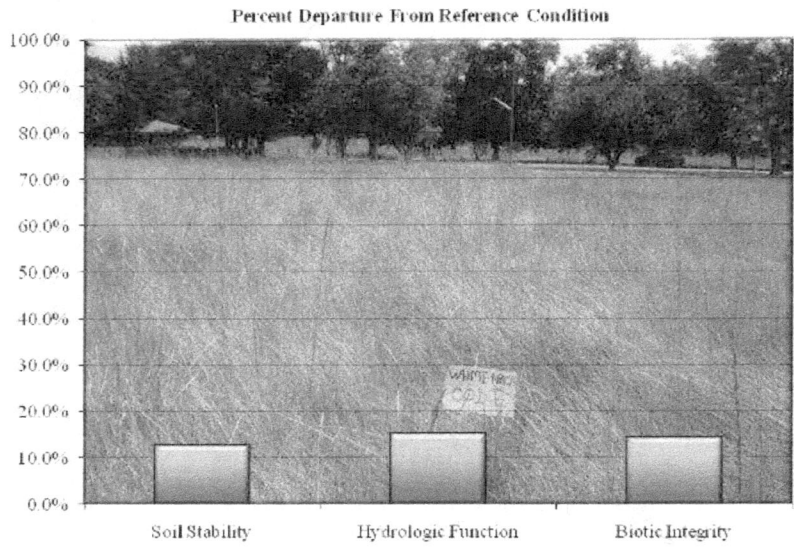

Figure 20. Departure from reference condition of the 3 landscape attributes in the Alkali Bottom 9-15PZ ecological site at VRM-D3, WHMI (background is of plot 1).

VRM – D4c

VRM – D4c is approximately 2.13 acres (2.25%) of WHMI located on the northwest corner of the park on the south side of Mill Creek and is very similar to VRM – D4b, which is .57 acres (.60%) and lies to the north of Mill Creek (Figure 21). The D4 unit was historically used as a pasture for livestock grazing, mainly cattle. Records indicate the unit has had no recent grazing and in 1986 a revegetation plan was implemented (Gilbert 1984). Garrett and Coyner (2003) documented less work completed in this unit than others in the park due to the lack of access by motorized equipment. The unit was treated with prescribed fire in 1987, but has had limited spraying or mowing since that time. The unit is a Catherine silt loam soil that is classified as a Wet Meadow 9-15PZ (R008XY601WA) ecological reference site. Based on the ecological reference site, the historical climax plant community is willow (Salix sp.)/bunchgrass/sedge (Carex spp.) and falls in the Columbia Basin Palouse Prairie Ecological System (NatureServe 2009).

One plot was evaluated in the unit (Figure 22). The soil stability and hydrologic function attributes were rated as none-slight departure (12.5% and 17.5%, respectively). The biotic integrity attribute was rated slight-moderate (34.3%) due to the presence of invasive plants. The site is dominated by Pacific willow (*Salix lasiandra*)/black cottonwood (*Populus balsamifera ssp. trichocarpa*) with an understory dominated by cheatgrass and reed canarygrass. The unit has converted from a shrub/grass dominated community to a tree-dominated community based on comparison to the ecological reference site. This may be due to the lack of natural wildfires over the past 150 years.

The unit is in relatively good condition for soil and hydrologic function and not a threat for soil erosion. The biotic function is in a similar condition to that documented in 1984 and 1985 (Gilbert 1984, Romo and Krueger 1985). There is still a variety of noxious weeds in the unit but herbicide spot spraying has reduced their cover and vigor. This unit is a lower priority for management being located in a little traveled portion of the park. The tree dominated cover meets the historical landscape objective. Recommendations are to continue current noxious weed management strategies and research potential native or non-native species that could be planted to compete with the noxious weeds.

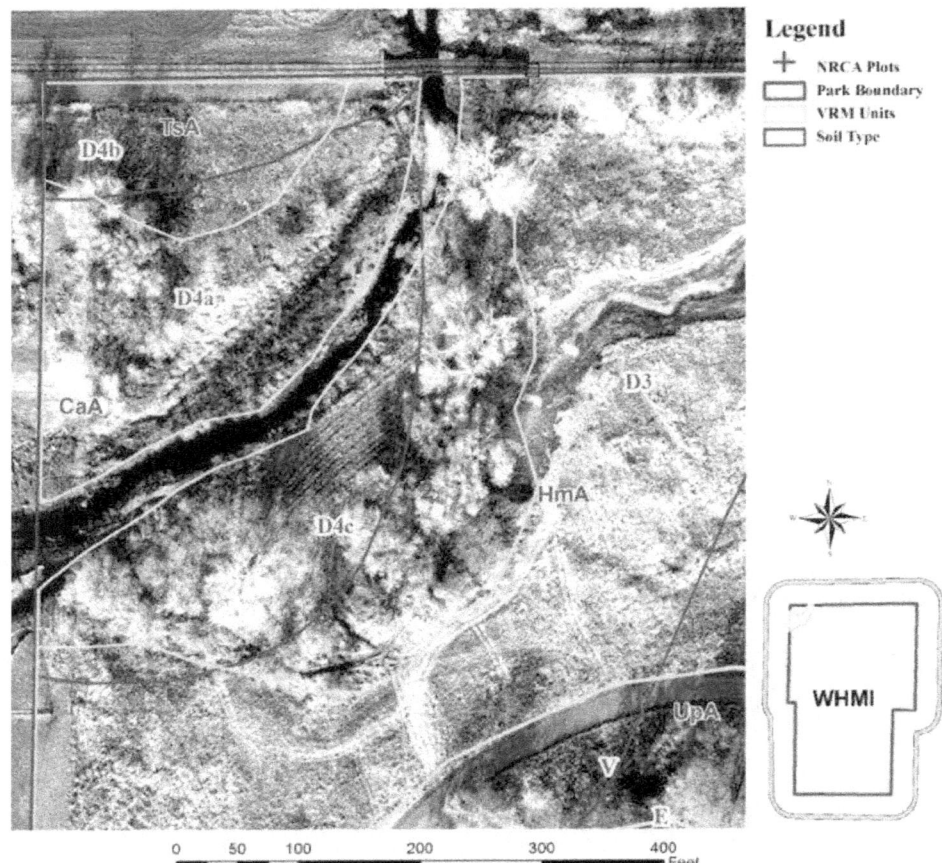

Figure 21. Map of VRM – D4c in WHMI.

Figure 22. Departure from reference condition of the 3 landscape attributes in the Wet Meadow 9-15PZ ecological site at VRM-D4c, WHMI (background is of plot 2).

38

VRM – F2

VRM – F2 is approximately 6.38 acres (6.76%) of WHMI located on the center west portion of the park and includes the core of the historical sites in the park (Figure 23). The site sampled is actually in the oxbow of the Walla Walla River and represents a semi-riparian community. The unit may have been historically used as pasture for livestock but has received very little use for several decades. The 1986 revegetation plan treated the oxbow areas in unit B but not the area in unit F2 (Gilbert 1984). Garrett and Coyner (2003) did not document work being completed in this portion of the unit. The unit is mapped as a Pedigo silt loam soil and is classified as an Alkali Bottom 15+PZ (R009XY401WA) ecological reference site. Based on the ecological reference site, the historical climax plant community is basin wildrye/bluebunch wheatgrass and falls in the Columbia Basin Palouse Prairie Ecological System (NatureServe 2009).

One plot was evaluated in the unit (Figure 24). The soil stability and hydrologic function attributes were rated as none-slight departure (2.5% and 7.5%, respectively). The biotic integrity attribute was also rated none-slight (17.1%). The biological integrity was in good condition but is not in a climax condition due to the presence of large willow, black cottonwoods, and black locust (*Robinia pseudoacacia*). The site is dominated by a dense stand of reed canarygrass which could imitate the historical stands of great basin wildrye along the Walla Walla River. Unfortunately, reed canarygrass is a state listed noxious weed and is a very aggressive competitor with native species in riparian areas.

The unit is in relatively good condition for all landscape attribute functions. The biotic function is in a similar condition to that documented in 1984 and 1985 (Gilbert 1984, Romo and Krueger 1985). There are a few of noxious weeds, except for reed canarygrass, in the unit but they are reduced in cover and vigor due to treatment with spot spraying, and shading from tree cover. This unit is a high priority for management and currently is meeting the historical landscape objective. Recommendations are to continue current noxious weeds management strategies and research methods for replacing reed canarygrass with a less aggressive species that meets the historical landscape criteria for the unit.

Figure 23. Map of VRM – F2 in WHMI.

Figure 24. Departure from reference condition of the 3 landscape attributes in the Alkali Bottom 15+PZ ecological site at VRM-F2, WHMI (background is of plot 6).

Aquatic Site Specific Assessments

Doan Creek

Doan Creek is a left bank, spring-fed tributary of Mill Creek located on WHMI (Figure 25). The Doan Creek irrigation ditch runs through WHMI and supplies water to the park and to two downstream irrigators. Overflow from the irrigation ditch supplies water to the Doan Creek channel that was relocated to its approximate historic channel location in the mid-1980s. Washington Department of Fish and Wildlife (WDFW) has documented that Doan Creek provides habitat for rainbow/steelhead trout (*Oncorhynchus mykiss*), speckled dace (*Rhinichthys osculus*), redside shiner (*Richardsonius balteatus*), 3 species of sculpins (*Cottus* spp.), and common carp (*Cyprinus carpio*) (NPS 2003). WDFW also anticipates that the restored habitat on the WHMI property can support Chinook salmon (*Oncorhynchus tshawytscha*) and coho salmon (*Oncorhynchus kisutch*).

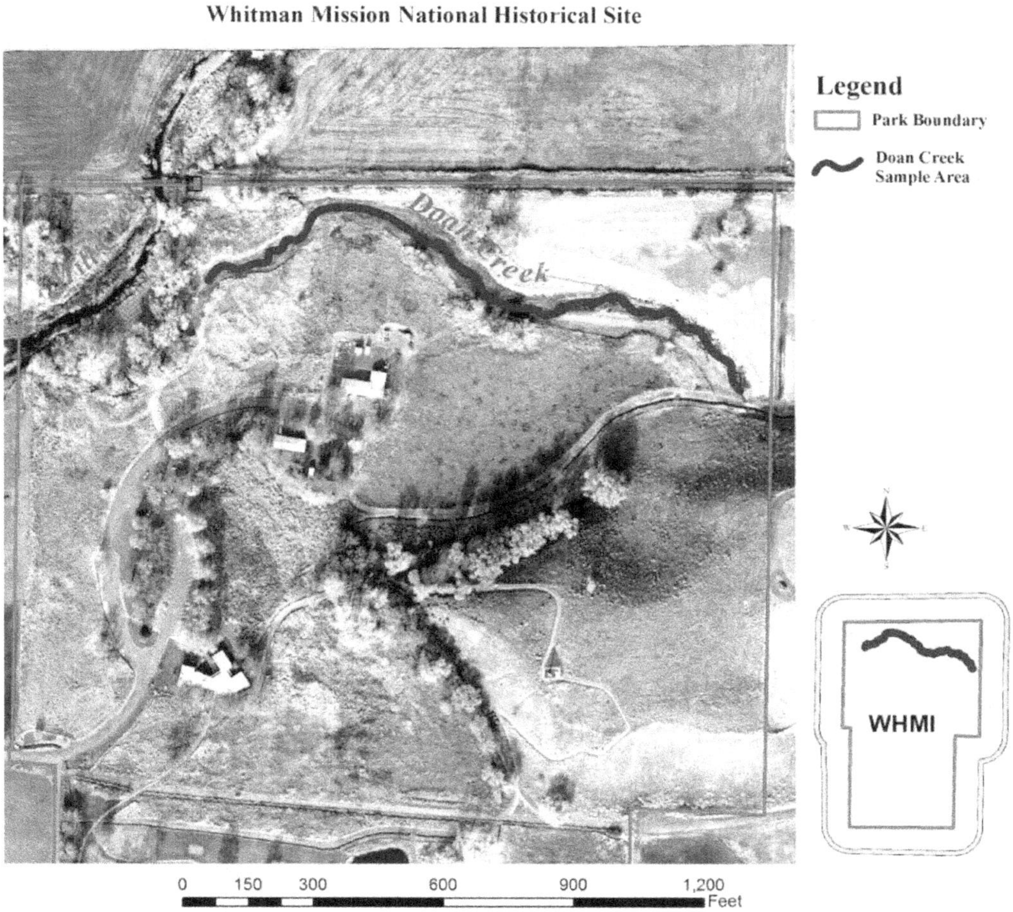

Figure 25. Map of the Doan Creek assessment reach in WHMI.

Restoration efforts of the original Doan Creek channel began in 2004 and restored Doan Creek to roughly its original water course between the park's eastern water diversion box and Mill Creek (NPS 2003). The stream channel now flows across the northwest border of the park and enters Mill Creek 300 feet south of the park's northwest border. The entire restored waterway contains natural meanderings in order to provide habitat suitable for the reintroduction of fish species to

41

the creek. The total length of the restored stream with meanderings is approximately 2500 feet. Stabilizing structures engineered with rock and wood materials have been installed at points where the slope of the channel exceeds -1% to slow the flow of water and dissipate energy. The WDFW habitat biologist helped design this restoration alternative as the optimal choice for fish habitat within WHMI and concluded there is a high chance that hatchery-reared or native fish would enter, survive, and spawn in Doan Creek as a result of the restoration activities (NPS 2003).

During the May 2008 field assessment, Doan Creek did not have water flow due to irrigation withdrawals upstream of the restored reach. However, in the late summer of 2008, a new irrigation pump was installed at the downstream end of the restored Doan Creek channel, which allows stream flows to persist in the restored channel rather than being diverted upstream (Figure 26). The goal is to maintain some streamflow in the active restored reach throughout the year and to re-establish potential fish passage from Mill Creek to Doan Creek.

Figure 26. Photograph of the water diversion pump near the mouth of Doan Creek at WHMI.

Doan Creek is associated with a large, offsite emergent wetland near the upstream portion of the restored reach on the northern edge of the WHMI property. This wetland extends to the northeast and presents an opportunity for wetland restoration efforts with the neighboring land owner.

Doan Creek is a relatively low gradient stream, which allows potential access to its floodplain. In addition, stream sinuosity resulting from restoration activities is sufficient to provide access to the floodplain and to promote active channel meandering. However, because Doan Creek is a spring-fed system and is largely controlled by irrigation withdrawals, high streamflow events appear to occur at a relatively infrequent basis. This low flooding frequency limits the extent of the existing riparian area and the potential for riparian expansion; however, the associated wetland that extends northward from the upstream portion of the restored reach provides an opportunity for sufficient hydrology to expand at least a portion of the riparian area.

Vegetation on Doan Creek is dominated by willow stake plantings resulting from recent revegetation efforts. Until recently, the site was dominated by reed canary grass, which is currently being treated through the use of a black plastic ground cover material allowing newly planted native vegetation to establish while helping to minimize reed canary grass seed germination. The willow stakes and newly emerging herbaceous vegetation along the stream appear vigorous and capable of withstanding any high streamflow events; however, much of the existing stream bank contains little, if any, ground cover and is susceptible to erosion until the plantings establish. Other than the engineered large woody debris used in restoring the stream channel, sources of large woody debris are lacking and will not be available until the newly planted woody vegetation matures significantly.

The existing Doan Creek channel characteristics are adequate to dissipate the generally low volume of flow that is conveyed through the channel. This is primarily due to the recent restoration activities. A sinuous stream channel has been created through the use of large woody debris and rock that provides a vertically stable stream with natural lateral movement and sediment processing.

The PFC evaluation of the Doan Creek stream reach on the WHMI property resulted in a summary determination of "Functional – At Risk" (Appendix A). This determination means that the riparian areas are in functional condition, but an existing soil, water, vegetation, or related attribute makes them susceptible to degradation. Since the Doan Creek channel is in the process of being restored on the WHMI property, it is well on its way to becoming properly functioning; however, channels that have recently been restored are often susceptible to damaging high flows and potential erosion due to newly emerging, immature riparian vegetation growth along the stream banks. Doan Creek will need several years of natural flows to establish a healthy equilibrium and become properly functioning. In particular, the stream system will need to experience more channel forming flows and establish a healthy density of riparian vegetation to transition to a balanced stream capable of processing sediment, minimizing onsite erosion, and dissipating flows.

Mill Creek
Mill Creek, a tributary to the Walla Walla River, originates on the western slopes of the Blue Mountains in southeastern Washington at an elevation of 5,500 feet (USACE 1995). It flows for 15 miles in a relatively deep and narrow canyon through mountainous terrain, before entering an alluvial fan a few miles east of the City of Walla Walla. Mill Creek enters the Walla Walla River about 6 miles west of the city at River Mile (RM) 33.6. Just upstream of Mill Creek's confluence with the Walla Walla River, it flows through the northern corner of the WHMI where it collects streamflow from Doan Creek (Figure 27). At this location and throughout the alluvial fan described above, Mill Creek flows through irrigated agriculture land and provides a large source of irrigation water to local farm fields. To accommodate farming, Mill Creek has been channelized or confined through the use of levees and/or rip rap. This channel confinement results in limited floodplain interaction, which prevents typical energy dissipation expected in a

natural stream system. Levees and rip rap banks have also limited lateral movement of the channel and have minimized the potential extent of the Mill Creek riparian area.

Whitman Mission National Historical Site

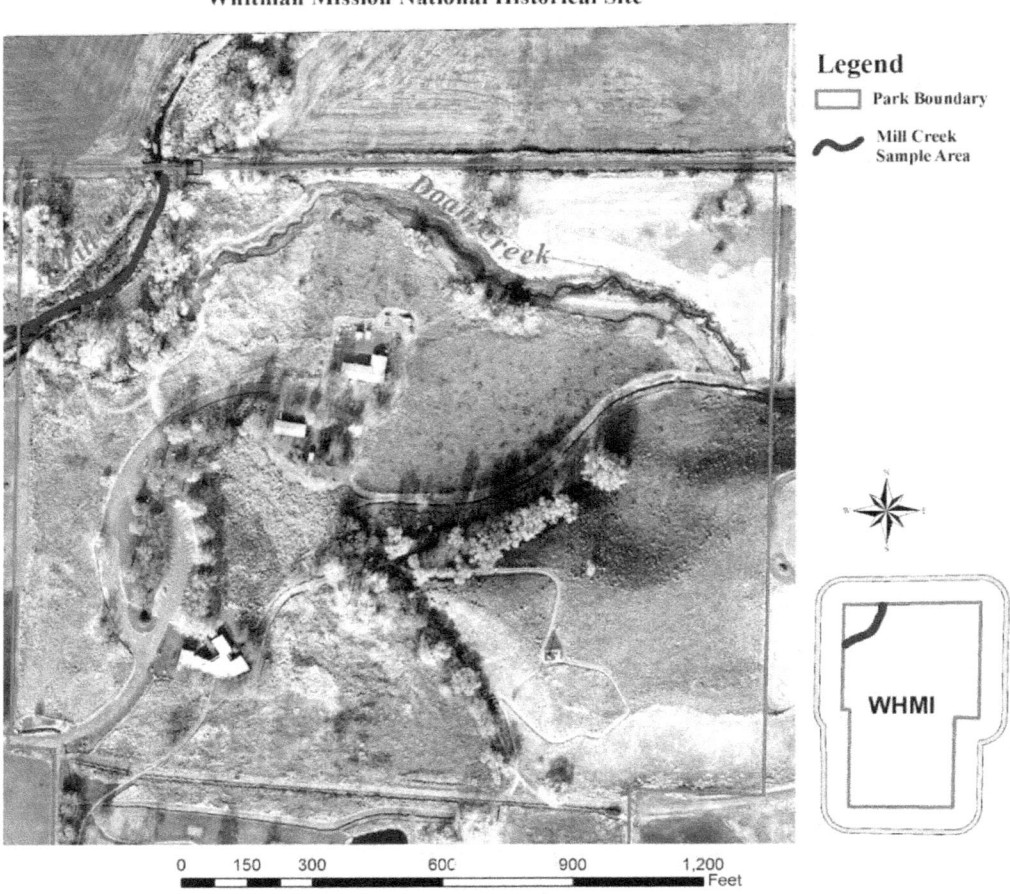

Figure 27. Map of the Mill Creek assessment reach at WHMI.

Onsite riparian vegetation consists of a narrow strip of both young and mature willow and cottonwood trees as well as dense coverage of invasive species, including reed canarygrass, which is preventing native understory colonization (Figure 28). The existing riparian vegetation lacks the diversity of native species and age classes necessary to maintain a healthy stream system onsite. The riparian vegetation that is present is vigorous and contains root masses capable of withstanding high streamflow events and protecting the stream banks from erosion, however, vegetative ground cover is inadequate to dissipate energy during high flows or provide sufficient large woody debris to the stream channel.

Figure 28. Photograph of Mill Creek assessment site at WHMI.

The large woody debris present in the onsite Mill Creek stream channel and associated riparian floodplain is inadequate to dissipate stream energy in a stream of this size. The lack of access to the floodplain also inhibits Mill Creek's ability to dissipate stream energy during high flows. Mill Creek contains a few small meanders but is limited in its movement due to the confining rip-rap stream banks and levees. Because stream energy cannot dissipate laterally, Mill Creek is vertically unstable and attempts to dissipate energy through down cutting on stream banks. Erosion is most likely due to farming. The railroad grade and trestle upstream do not seem to be a significant cause of erosion.

The PFC evaluation of the Mill Creek stream reach on the WHMI property resulted in a summary determination of "Functional – At Risk" (Appendix A). This determination means that the riparian areas are in functional condition, but an existing soil, water, vegetation, or related attribute makes them susceptible to degradation. The confinement of the Mill Creek channel (i.e., rip rap, earthen levees) creates an unnatural system that is susceptible to degradation. As a result, the stream is trending away from proper functioning condition and will continue trending downward unless channel confinement pressure is reduced through levee setback that allows natural stream sinuosity and floodplain connectivity to be re-established. In its current state, Mill Creek stream flow dissipation occurs in higher gradient reaches through down cutting, which results in vertical instability and potential mass wasting of the stream bank, further exacerbating the sediment problem in aggrading low gradient stream reaches. The most evident effects of sedimentation at the Mill Creek site include reductions in pool habitat, increased cobble embeddedness, lower salmonid reproductive success, and increased bank erosion due to forced lateral channel adjustment.

Mill Creek water quality monitoring conducted by Starkey (2009) in 2008 indicated the stream is in poor to fair condition. Water chemistry data were collected from May–October 2008 and compared with Washington Department of Ecology thresholds. Starkey (2009) indicated water chemistry parameters of primary concern at this site include high water temperatures, high pH, and low dissolved oxygen concentrations.

Benthic Macroinvertebrates

The majority of the substrate at the Mill Creek invertebrate assessment site was comprised of inorganic material (95%), while the remaining 5% of the material was organic in nature. The assessment team estimated that 25-30% of the substrate was comprised of fine sediments; however, cobbles appeared fairly clean of cemented sediments and had an estimated embeddedness of 10%. Stream shading at the invertebrate sampling site was estimated at 15% due to the prevalence of reed canary grass and other herbaceous vegetation along the stream bank rather than substantial overstory vegetation. Invertebrates were sampled from a 21.0 m long riffle averaging 0.3 m in depth, 2.0 m in width, and 0.8 m/sec surface velocity. At this location, the overall stream channel was 12.2 m in width.

Mill Creek received an Idaho Stream Macroinvertebrate Index (SMI) score of 28, corresponding to "poor" ecological conditions in the "Basins" region. Mill Creek received a similarly low Oregon IBI score of 16, suggesting "severely impaired" ecological conditions. These results indicate Mill Creek, as it flows through the WHMI property, is not currently supporting and maintaining a balanced community of organisms that has the composition, diversity, and functional organization comparable to that of a natural habitat within the same region.

Macroinvertebrate samples collected at the WHMI Mill Creek site by Starkey (2009) in 2008 indicate that the water quality within Mill Creek is fair. This result is based on general comparisons between onsite macroinvertebrate composition and the composition of comparable streams within the region utilizing a general index of integrity known as the Hilsenhoff Biotic Index (HBI). The HBI indicated organic pollution appears to significantly affect onsite water quality.

Perturbations occurring upstream of the sampling site are often the primary cause for poor conditions at the sampling site. While a single BMI sample is not enough to compare and contrast degradation occurring throughout the watershed, it can be used as a baseline measurement from which future BMI samples at the individual site can be compared. The comparison of B-IBI scores from year to year will help managers test the effectiveness of management actions occurring near the site and upstream in the watershed. It is always difficult to pinpoint the exact cause of ecological conditions at a site based on the B-IBI score; however, several common correlations exist between a B-IBI score and conditions or practices occurring within a watershed. B-IBI scores have been shown to positively correlate with vegetative cover, riparian tree density, water quantity and quality, and substrate particle size (EVS Environmental 2004). Conversely, a negative correlation is often evident between B-IBI scores and the amount of developed land or urbanization occurring upstream in the watershed. Observations of conditions within the Mill Creek watershed match closely with these correlations. Vegetative cover and riparian tree density have been reduced throughout the watershed over the past century to provide opportunities for agriculture (Barber 2005). Irrigation water withdrawals, agriculture practices, and urbanization have lead to poor water quantity and quality throughout Mill Creek

(USACE 1995). Land use throughout the watershed has resulted in increased erosion, which subsequently leads to sedimentation, cobble embeddedness, and reduced salmonid productivity. Urbanization and land development continue to occur upstream of the sampled Mill Creek site, which increases impervious surfaces and flashy tendencies of Mill Creek flows.

Threats and Stressors

Threats and stressors are defined as a condition or situation, occurrence, or factor causing a negative impact to a natural resource. These can be further divided into naturally occurring or human-caused depending on their source. This section reports on 3 upland and 5 aquatic threats and stressors. Climate change is treated as a threat to upland and aquatic natural resources.

Upland Resources

Upland resource threats at WHMI include wildfire, land use change, and noxious weeds. Each upland resource threat is described in more detail below including discussions of potential strategies to address upland resource risks.

Land Use Changes

The Walla Walla River Subbasin includes all or part of five counties in Washington and Oregon; Walla Walla and Columbia Counties in Washington and Umatilla, Union and Wallowa Counties in Oregon. WHMI is located in Walla Walla County and Table 8 is a summary of the population change in the county from 2000 to 2006 (U.S. Census Bureau 2007). Relative to the State of Washington, Walla Walla County is growing more slowly than the State and has a lower population density. Development is much lower than the state average relative to building permits issued on a per capita basis.

Table 8. Demographics for the Walla Wall County in the WHMI project area.

| County | State | Population | | | Persons /mi[2] | BP[1] 2006 | BP[1] /1000 people | Size - mi[2] |
		2000	2006	% Change				
Walla Walla	Washington	55,180	57,721	4.6%	43.4	290	0.20	1,270
	Washington	5,894,121	6,395,798	8.5%	88.6	50,033	7.82	66,544

[1] Building Permits

Walla Walla County projects a population of 15,792 by 2025 in the rural areas of the county based on the 2004 population of 12,462 and a 1.34% annual growth rate (WWCBC 2007). Of benefit to WHMI, is the policy of Walla Walla County to direct most growth into urban growth areas. Unfortunately, all of the urban growth areas lie upstream from WHMI and could potentially impact the quantity and/or quality of water in Mill Creek. WHMI staff will need to work closely with Walla Walla County staff and adjacent landowners to maintain the visual landscape outside the park boundaries in order to meet the objectives established in the General Management Plan.

Noxious Weeds

Romo and Krueger (1985) developed a list of 6 noxious weeds for WHMI and recommended different control and revegetation methods. WHMI staff conducted a noxious weed inventory in 1997 and identified4 species noted by Romo and Krueger (1985) and 2 new species (NPS 2000). Garrett et al. (2007) developed a list of important noxious and non-native plant species based on the knowledge of NPS park staff while developing the UCBN Inventory and Monitoring Plan. This report identified 4 of the species from the 1997 list and added an additional 3 noxious weed species to those previously identified as important. During site specific field work for this report only one additional species, bull thistle (*Cirsium vulgare*), was identified that was not previously mentioned in the above reports.

Table 9 is a list of noxious and invasive plant species referenced in the previous reports. There have been 12 species listed at least once since 1985 that were identified as important to control at WHMI. In addition there are 3 noxious weed species not mentioned in any reports but found in the plant species list maintained by the UCBN; hoary cress (*Cardaria draba*), spotted knapweed (*Centaurea maculosa*), and diffuse knapweed (*Centaurea diffusa*).

Washington State's Noxious Weed law classifies noxious weeds into one of 3 categories; Class A, B, or C (WSNWCB 2009). Class A species (35 spp.) are limited in distribution and are the highest priority for prevention and eradication. Class B species (71 spp.) are limited in distribution within one or more of the 10 regions in the state. Class C species (31 spp.) are considered widespread in the state and control requirements are determined by each county. County weed control boards are required to list the Class B species that must be contained to prevent further spread. Walla Walla County is located in Region 10 and Table 9 includes the 42 Class B species identified as a priority by the Walla Walla County Weed Control Board. Currently, only 2 speciesof the 42-Class B species listed by Walla Walla County Weed Board, diffuse and spotted knapweed, have been identified in WHMI.

In 2002, the UCBN created a database management system for tracking noxious weed control efforts at WHMI called the Integrated Pest Management Geodatabase (IPMG). The IPMG used ArcGIS software to map and managed data collected by WHMI staff. The data was maintained from 2002 to 2005. The dataset was summarized by year to provide an estimate of the level of effort being exerted by WHMI staff to control noxious weeds on the 98.15 acres of the park. Figure 29 is a graph of the number of acres treated by species and year from 2002 to 2005. Total acres treated by year was 34.33 acres (2002), 26.88 acres (2003, 74.37 acres (2004), and 49.79 acres (2005). The areas treated are displayed in Figure 30.

Invasive and noxious weeds are a major threat to WHMI cultural and natural resources. WHMI weed control efforts since 1985 have improved many of the VRM units in the park. Some VRM units still require extensive work to achieve the stated objective of restoring and maintaining the historical landscape. Good management will require the continuation of the extensive levels of effort to control noxious weeds and to revegetate areas dominated by undesirable species. WHMI staff will need to continue working closely with other agencies and local landowners to protect from the many invasive species found in surrounding areas.

Table 9. List of noxious and non-native weeds in WHMI with an 'x' indicating the source and the ranking by the state of Washington.

Common Name	Scientific Name	Washington State Class	Romo and Krueger 1985	Inventory 1997	Monitoring Plan 2007	NRCA Plots 2008	Species List	Walla Walla County
Quackgrass	Elymus repens		X				X	
Poison Hemlock	Conium maculatum	B	X	X	X	X	X	
Spikeweed	Hemizonia pungens	C			X	X	X	
Diffuse Knapweed	Centaurea diffusa	B	X				X	
Yellow Starthistle	Centaurea solstitialis	B	X	X	X	X	X	
Canada Thistle	Cirsium arvense	C	X	X	X	X	X	
Field bindweed	Convuvulus arvensis	C		X		X	X	
Kochia	Kochia scoparia	B			X		X	
Scotch thistle	Onopordum acanthium	B	X	X	X	X	X	
Jointed goatgrass	Aegilops cylindrica	C		X			X	
Canary Reed Grass	Phalaris arundinacea	C			X	X	X	
Bull Thistle	Cirsium vulgare	C				X	X	
Hoarycress	Cardaria draba	C					X	
Spotted Knapweed	Centaurea maculosa	B					X	X
Common Bugloss	Anchusa officinalis	B						X
Dalmatian Toadflax	Linaria genistifolia	B						X
Austrian fieldcress	Rorippa austriaca	B						X
Blackgrass	Alopecurus myosuroides	B						X
Blueweed	Echium vulgare	B						X
Camelthorn	Alhagi maurorum	B						X
Common Catsear	Hypochaeris radicata	B						X
Common Fennel	Foeniculum vulgare	B						X
Smooth Cordgrass	Apartina alterniflora	B						X
Fanwort	Cabomba caroliniana	B						X
Gorse	Ulex europaeus	B						X
Oxtongue Hawkweed	Picris hieracioides	B						X
Mouseear Hawkweed	Hieracium pilosella	B						X
Orange Hawkweed	Hieracium aurantiacum	B						X
Polar Hawkweed	Hieracium atratum	B						X
Smooth Hawkweed	Hieracium laevigatum	B						X
Yellow Hawkweed	Hieracium caespitosum	B						X
Robert Herb	Geranium robertianum	B						X
Indigobush	Amorpha fruticosa	B						X
Black Knapweed	Centaurea nigra	B						X
Brown Knapweed	Centaureau jacea	B						X

Table 9. (continued)

Common Name	Scientific Name	Washington State Class	Romo and Krueger 1985	Inventory 1997	Monitoring Plan 2007	NRCA Plots 2008	Species List	Walla Walla County
Meadow Knapweed	Centaureau jacea x nigra	B						X
Russian Knapweed	Acroptilon repens	B					X	X
Lepyrodiclis	Lepyrodiclis holosteoides	B						X
Oxeye Daisy	Leucanthemum vulgare	B						X
Parrotfeather	Myriophyllum aquaticum	B						X
Perennial Pepperweed	Lepidium latifolium	B						X
Policeman's Helmet	Impateins glandulifera	B						X
Scotch Broom	Cytisus scoparius	B						X
Laurel Spurge	Daphne laureola	B						X
Leafy Spurge	Euphorbia esula	B						X
Sulfur Cinquefoil	Potentilla recta	B						X
Swainsonpea	Sphaerophysa salsula	B						X
Tansy Ragwort	Senecio jacobaea	B						X
Musk Thistle	Carduus nutans	B						X
Plumeless Thistle	Carduus acanthoides	B						X
Water Primrose	Ludwigia hexapetala	B						X
Wild Chervil	Anthriscus sylvestris	B						X
Yellow Floating Heart	Nymphoides peltata	B						X
Yellow nutsedge	Cyperus esculentus	B						X

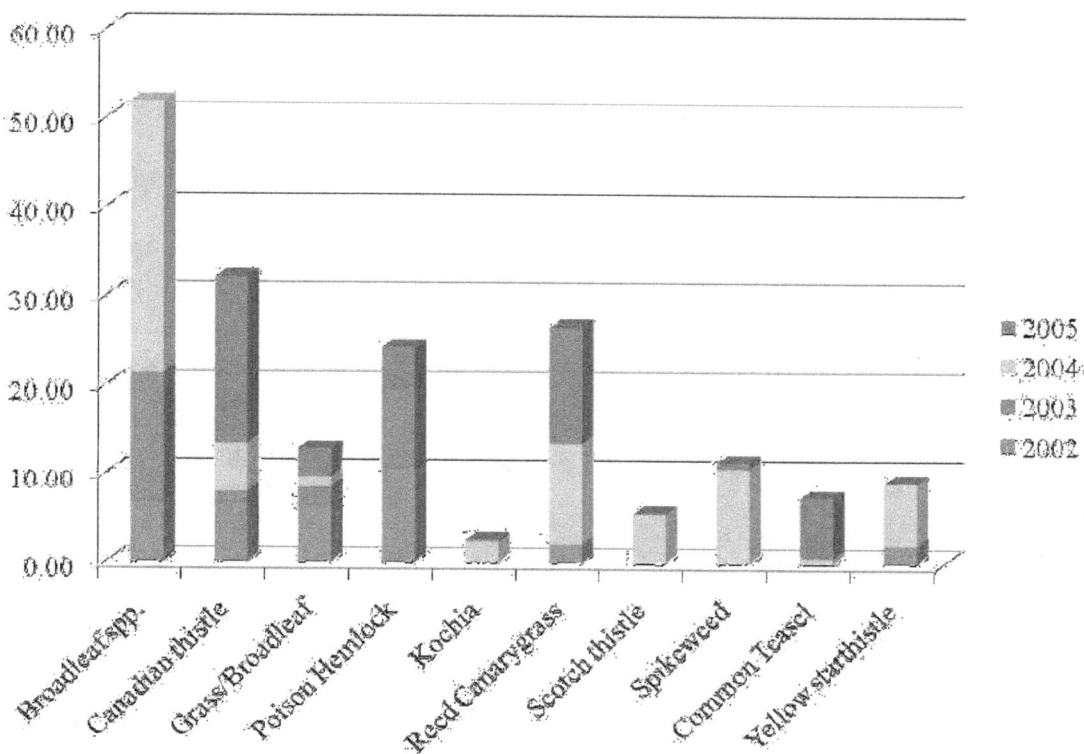

Figure 29. Graph of treated acres by species at WHMI from 2002-2005.

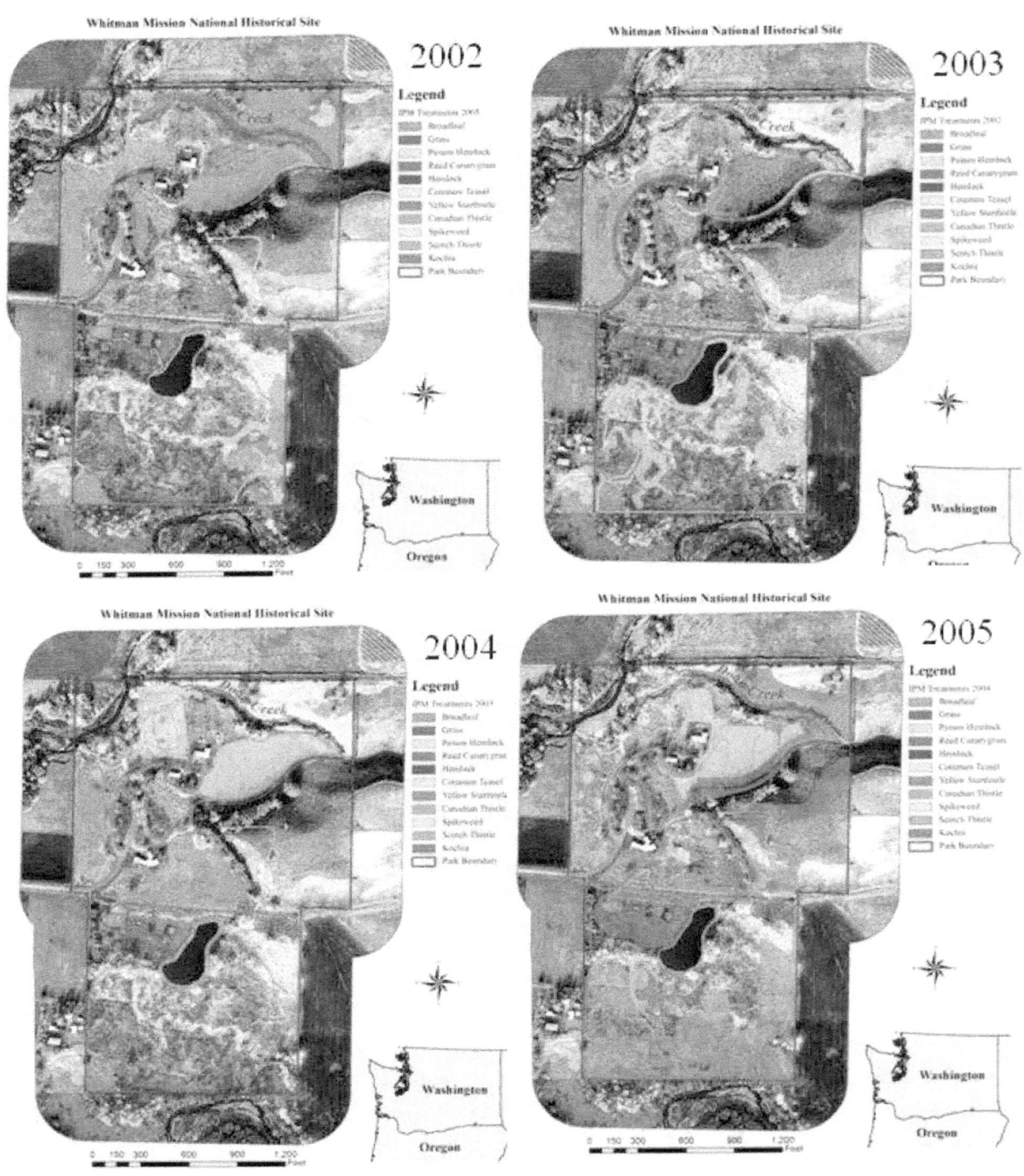

Figure 30. Maps of IPM treatments for weeds by year at WHMI from 2002-2005.

Aquatic Resources
Aquatic resource threats at WHMI include invasive riparian species, recreational use, water quantity and quality, fine sediments, and land use. Each aquatic resource threat is described in more detail below in addition to discussions of potential strategies to address the risks that are threatening aquatic resources.

Invasive riparian species
Reed canarygrass dominates Mill Creek's stream banks. Reed canarygrass is a concern because it forms large, single-species stands that prevents establishment of other species. Since restoration of Doan Creek started, invasive plant species have been prevented from establishing in the project area and constant management will be required to maintain this condition. Prevention of new reed canarygrass invasions is the most efficient and cost effective invasive species management. Prevention of reed canarygrass can be most efficiently accomplished by maintaining complex native herbaceous canopies. Reed canarygrass seed germination requires light penetration to the soil surface, which is prevented by shade from trees and shrubs.

Recreational use
Recreational use in the vicinity of Mill Creek and Doan Creek on the WHMI property is a common occurrence due to tourists visiting the park each year. It is important to manage use of the onsite aquatic resources in a way that educates the public without compromising the integrity of the resource. This can be accomplished by ensuring healthy vegetated riparian buffers exist around Mill and Doan Creek to protect instream resources from surrounding land use impacts. Park managers should also educate the public about the importance of restricting access within riparian areas and staying on park trails. An educational riparian area sign and platform that allows tourists to view the newly emerging Doan Creek riparian area would be good additions to the park.

Water quantity and quality
Water withdrawals for irrigation reduce water quantity and are a critical concern for Mill Creek and Doan Creek, especially during the late summer. Water quantity can limit fish production due to reduced fish passage, spawning habitat, and rearing habitat. Water quality is often tied to water quantity, especially in the arid regions of the western U.S. This is the case for Mill Creek and Doan Creek. Water temperatures are regulated by the quantity of water flowing in a stream channel and have been reported as a problem in these watersheds (Barber 2005). High water temperatures can also inhibit a stream's ability to produce salmonid species, which require cool, clean water during all phases of their life history. In addition, fecal coliform bacteria problems within streams are often exacerbated by low flows and high stream temperatures. To address water quantity and quality concerns, it is recommended that managers prioritize maintenance of natural flows as much as possible during the summer low flow period (July – October).

Fine sediments
High sediment loading is one of the habitat factors identified as limiting salmonid productivity in the Mill Creek watershed (Barber 2005). Fines deposited on streambeds after salmonids have spawned reduce the survival from egg to fry if levels are excessive. Fine sediment also affects the number and diversity of invertebrates, which provides an important food resource for salmonids. Fine material is generally produced in the uplands, transported to a stream, and is either deposited on the banks or enters the stream. As channels migrate laterally, streambanks are

eroded and fine material enters the stream. Fine materials in the stream often lead to cobble embeddedness, which results in reduced salmonid productivity.

Timber harvest, grazing, agricultural practices, development and cut banks along roadways have all resulted in accelerated sediment production and delivery to the greater Walla Walla River basin's surface waters compared to historic conditions (Barber 2005). It is difficult to manage sediment loading onsite that is occurring as a result of upstream land use activities. It is possible to help control and prevent fine sediments from entering Mill and Doan Creeks on the WHMI property. In some cases, particularly in smaller streams like Doan Creek, wood can be used to retain sediment (creating step pools along steeper gradient reaches), promote bed and bank stability, and thereby reduce the volume of sediment delivered to downstream reaches. Another effective way to reduce non-point sources of sediment on the WHMI property is to ensure densely vegetated riparian buffers exist to trap sediments prior to delivery to the stream. Much of the sediment problem in the Mill Creek watershed is due to channelization of the stream from agricultural activities adjacent to stream banks. Levee setback on the WHMI property would be another way to allow some natural sediment processing to occur onsite. Levee setback would allow the stream to laterally migrate and deposit sediments into a network of secondary channels, off-channel habitat, and/or a floodplain bench during high flows.

Land use
Agricultural activities in the Mill Creek watershed throughout the last century have resulted in channelization of the stream, loss of floodplain habitat, and a reduction in vegetative density and overall width of riparian areas. In addition, urbanization and land development in the greater Walla Walla region is occurring, which exacerbates water quality problems and often results in flashy stream flows due to the increased rate of storm water runoff. Mill Creek on the WHMI property is channelized and could be improved by setting back levees to allow for natural stream processes to occur (e.g., floodplain connection, sediment processing, fish habitat development, etc.). Widening riparian areas and increasing riparian plant density would also help cool stream water (through shading and groundwater reconnection) and minimize delivery of onsite fine sediment to the stream.

Climate Change
The Intergovernmental Panel on Climate Change (IPCC) is a scientific intergovernmental body set up by the World Meteorological Organization and by the United Nations Environment Program. The IPCC Working Group II focuses on climate change impacts, adaptation, and vulnerability. Parry et al. (2007) published a technical summary of their most recent findings. Listed below are a few of the notable findings from the report:

- Observational evidence from all continents and most oceans show that many natural systems are being affected by regional climate changes, particularly temperature increases.
- A global assessment of data since 1970 has shown it is likely that anthropogenic warming has had a discernible influence on many physical and biological systems.
- Other effects of regional climate changes on natural and human environments are emerging, although many are difficult to discern due to adaptation and non-climatic drivers.

- Some large-scale climate events have the potential to cause very large impacts, especially after the 21st century.
- Impacts of climate change will vary regionally but, aggregated and discounted to the present, they are very likely to impose net annual costs, which will increase over time as global temperatures increase.
- Vulnerability to climate change can be exacerbated by the presence of other stresses.
- Future vulnerability depends not only on climate change but also on development pathway.
- Many impacts can be avoided, reduced, or delayed by mitigation.

The IPCC Working Group II published reports on many areas of the world. North America was addressed by Field et al. (2007) and they documented three observable connections between climate change and terrestrial ecosystems. They found changes in seasonal timing of life-cycle events and phenology, plant growth or primary production, and biogeographic distribution. They also noted that direct impacts on organisms have indirect effects on ecological mechanisms (competition, herbivory, disease) and disturbance (wildfire, hurricanes, human activities).

Plants green-up and flower earlier in the spring and leaf fall occurs later in the fall. Primary production has increased in North American forests over the past 10 years (Boisvenue and Running 2006). Nesting and breeding occurs earlier, migration is earlier for migratory species, and some species are shifting home ranges to higher elevations or to more northern latitudes. A warming climate encourages wildfires through a longer summer period that further reduces fuel moisture promoting easier ignition and faster spread (Running 2006). Westerling et al. (2006) found that in the last three decades the wildfire season in the western U.S. has increased by 78 days and burn durations of fires greater than 1,000 hectares in area have increased from 7.5 to 37.1 days, in response to a spring/summer warming of 0.87°C.

The Joint Institute for the Study of Atmosphere and Oceans (JISAO) is a cooperative institute between the National Oceanic and Atmospheric Administration (NOAA) and the University of Washington. JISAO has published a report titled "Impacts of climate variability and change in the Pacific Northwest" (Mote et al. 2005). Their modeling predicts warmer, wetter winters, an increase of 3.1° F. by 2030 and a 5% increase in precipitation. Precipitation would come more in the form of rain with smaller snow packs.

The predicted climate changes project little change in the annual flow of the Columbia River, but seasonal flows will shift markedly toward larger winter and spring flows and smaller summer and autumn flows (Hamlet and Lettenmaier, 1999). The changes in flows will likely coincide with increased water demand, principally from regional growth, but also induced by climate change. Climate change is also projected to impact urban water supplies within the basin. For example, a 2°C warming projected for the 2040s would increase demand for water in Portland, Oregon by 1.5 billion gallons per year with an additional demand of 5.5 billion gallons per year from population growth, while decreasing supply by 1.3 billion gallons per year (Mote et al., 2003). The 43 sub-basins in the Columbia River basin have their own sub-basin management plans for fish and wildlife, but none comprehensively addresses reduced summertime flows caused by climate change.

The direct and indirect impact of these predicted changes in climate on natural resources at WHMI is a complex and difficult issue to address. Changes could be positive or negative depending on the ecosystem processes, communities, and/or species under consideration. WHMI managers should review which plant and animal communities and/or species of special interest and address the possible impacts of the predicted changes in climate to each on individually. Where possible, plans could be developed to mitigate potential negative impacts to communities and/or species.

Summary and Recommendations

Upland Resources

This report examined 7 site-specific areas in WHMI vegetation restoration management units using a rapid resource assessment methodology (Pellant 2005). The results and recommendations for each site is found in the results section of this report. General threats/stressors thought to be the most important to management of WHMI's natural resources were examined using available information. These were land use change and noxious weeds for upland habitats and water level fluctuations, invasive riparian species, recreational use, water quality, and fine sediments for aquatic habitats. Climate change was considered capable of affecting both habitats.

Due to the lack of consistent quantitative information on these threats/stressors, impacts were evaluated in a qualitative manner. Table 10 is an overall estimate of the potential impact to the 3 major resource areas; soil, hydrologic, and biotic. The actual impact from these threats/stressors to any specific site will vary depending on the existing natural resource and landscape setting.

Table 10. Potential impact from selected threats/stressors to the major resources/processes at WHMI.

Threats/Stressors	Major Resources/Processes		
Upland Habitats	Soils	Hydrologic	Biotic
Land use change			
Noxious weeds			
Aquatic Habitats			
Invasive Riparian Species			
Recreational Use			
Water Quantity and Quality			
Fine Sediments			
All Habitats			
Climate Change			
Key to Rating for Threats/Stressors			
Potential impact to resource	High	Moderate	Low

Table 11 is a summary of the potential impacts to WHMI natural resources from the threats/stressors identified by Garrett et al. (2007). Rankings were based on literature and database research and are the professional judgment of the authors. There is, in fact, very little documented information available to assess possible threats/stressors to WHMI natural resources.

Data Gaps

Many types of information were not available for this report. We have summarized important data that would improve natural resource management by WHMI staff. We did not estimate cost or indicate agency responsibility due to the extensive nature of the data. This report will hopefully provide guidance to WHMI staff on future data collection efforts within and outside the park. Below is a list of the major data gaps:

1. Accurate and standardized land cover/use mapping for the project area that meets National Map Accuracy Standards (± 40') and is repeatable over time. This information is very important for any watershed modeling of water quality attributes and other resource values. The NPS Inventory and Monitoring Program is currently researching methods to standardized developing land use maps for long term monitoring.
2. Land ownership maps in digital format, like county parcel maps, with information on owner name and address and any records on what has been developed on the parcel. This information could allow WHMI staff to be proactive in monitoring land development adjacent to the park in a cost efficient and timely manner. Data is currently available online at http://wallawallawa.taxsifter.com/taxsifter/t-parcelsearch.asp but was not available digitally.
3. Noxious weed maps in digital format on adjacent private and public lands within the project boundary. Currently, no county, state, federal, or other organization collect and map noxious weed locations in the WHMI project area. Managers would be more aware of possible new invaders and could develop better management strategies for existing species with this information. County and state agencies have legal requirements for tracking noxious weeds and would be the best partners for developing this information in digital format.

Table 11. Matrix of threats/stressors to major resources areas with ratings for potential impacts and the knowledge base for estimates in WHMI.

Threats/Stressors	Major Resources/Processes			
Natural Disturbances	Soils	Hydrologic	Biotic	Air
Wildfires	2	2	1	3
Flooding	3	3	3	3
Drought	4	3	2	4
Landslides	2	1	4	4
Exotic diseases	4	4	2	4
Climate Change	4	2	3	4
Human-cause Disturbances				
Invasive plants/noxious weeds	2	2	1	4
Livestock grazing	1	1	1	4
Fire management practices	3	2	1	2
NPS management activities	3	3	3	4
Forest management practices	2	1	1	4
Visitor use	3	2	1	3
Landscape/landuse changes	2	1	2	3
Exotic animals	4	4	1	3
Hunting	4	4	2	4
Rural development	3	2	2	4
Air pollution	3	3	4	2
Water pollution	4	1	1	4
Utilities/industry	3	2	2	2
Air traffic	4	4	3	3
Heavy metal contamination	2	1	2	4

Key to Rating for Threats/Stressors				
Potential impact to resource	High	Moderate	Low	Unknown
Knowledge Base	1 = Good	2 = Fair	3 = Poor	4=Inferential

Literature Cited

Anglin, Donald, Darren Gallion, Marshall Barrows, Coutney Newlon, and Ryan Koch. 2008. Current Status of Bull Trout Abundance, Connectivity, and Habitat Conditions in the Walla Walla Basin. U.S. Fish and Wildlife Service.

Barber, Mike. 2005. Walla Walla Watershed WRIA 32 Level 1 Assessment. Economic and Engineering Services, Inc.

Boisvenue, C. and S.W. Running, 2006: Impacts of climate change on natural forest productivity - evidence since the middle of the 20th century. Global Change Biololgy, 12, 862-882.

Bonneville Power Administration. 2004. Walla Walla Subbasin Plan. Northwest Power Planning Council. Portland, Oregon.

Comer, P., D. Faber-Langendoen, R. Evans, S. Gawler, C. Josse, G. Kittel, S. Menard, M. Pyne, M. Reid, K. Schulz, K. Snow, and J. Teague. 2003. Ecological Systems of the United States: A Working Classification of U.S. Terrestrial Systems. NatureServe, Arlington, Virginia

Environnemental Systems Research Institute. 2006. ArcGIS 9, Using ArcGIS Desktop. Environnemental Systems Research Institute

Field, C.B., L.D. Mortsch,, M. Brklacich, D.L. Forbes, P. Kovacs, J.A. Patz, S.W. Running and M.J. Scott. 2007. North America. Climate Change 2007: Impacts, Adaptation and Vulnerability. Contribution of Working Group II to the Fourth Assessment Report of the Intergovernmental Panel on Climate Change, M.L. Parry, O.F. Canziani, J.P. Palutikof, P.J. van der Linden and C.E. Hanson, Eds., Cambridge University Press, Cambridge, UK, 617-652.

Garrett, L. K. and J. Coyner. 2003. History of Vegetation Restoration, Whitman Mission National Historic Site. Cooperative Agreement No. CA9000-95-018, National Park Service, Fort Collins, Colorado

Garrett, L. K., T. J. Rodhouse, G. H. Dicus, C. C. Caudill, and M. R. Shardlow. 2007. Upper Columbia Basin Network vital signs monitoring plan. Natural Resource Report NPS/UCBN/NRR—2007/002. National Park Service, Fort Collins, Colorado.

Gilbert, C. A. 1984. Landscape Study and Management Alternatives for Revegetation Whitman Mission National Historic Site. National Park Service, Pacific Northwest Region, Cultural Resources Division.

Hamlet, A. and D. Lettenmaier. 1999. Effects of climate change on hydrology and water resources in the Columbia River Basin. Journal of American Water Resources Association, 35, 1597-1623.

Mahoney, Brian, Craig Contor, Stacy Schumacher, and Jesse Schwartz. 2007. Fluvial Movement of Radio Tagged Adult Bull Trout in the Walla Walla River, northeastern Oregon - Draft. Confederated Tribes of the Umatilla Indian Reservation and Oregon Department of Fish and Wildlife.

Mahoney, Brian, Michael Lambert, Preston Bronson, Travis Olsen, and Jesse Schwartz. 2007. Walla Walla Basin Natural Production Monitoring and Evaluation Project. Confederated Tribes of the Umatilla Indian Reservation and Walla Walla Community College, Prepared for US Department of Energy.

National Park Service (NPS). 2000. General Management Plan for Whitman Mission National Historic Site. U.S. Department of Interior, National Park Service.

National Park Service (NPS). 2008. Whitman Mission National Historic Site Doan Creek Restoration Project Environmental Assessment. Online. http://www.nps.gov/archive/whmi/manage/doancreek/doancreek.htm#tc. Accessed 1 January 2009.

Natural Resource Conservation Service (NRCS). 2008. Walla Walla County *electronic* Field Office Technical Guide. Online. http://efotg.nrcs.usda.gov/treemenuFS.aspx. Accessed 1 January 2009.

NatureServe. 2009. NatureServe Explorer – Ecological Communities and Systems. U.S. Geologic
Survey. Online. http://www.NatureServe.org/explorer/servlet/NatureServe?init=Ecol. Accessed 1 January 2009.

Pacific Groundwater Group. 1995. Initial Watershed Assessment Water Resources Inventory Area 22 Walla Walla River Watershed. Open-File Technical Report 95-11. Walla Walla Watershed Initial Assessment, Draft 1995, WR-95-159.

Parry, M.L., O.F. Canziani, J.P. Palutikof and Co-authors. 2007. Technical Summary. Climate Change 2007: Impacts, Adaptation and Vulnerability. Contribution of Working Group II to the Fourth Assessment Report of the Intergovernmental Panel on Climate Change, M.L. Parry, O.F. Canziani, J.P. Palutikof, P.J. van der Linden and C.E. Hanson, Eds., Cambridge University Press, Cambridge, UK, 23-78.

Pyke, D. A., J. E. Herrick, P. Shaver, and M. Pellant. 2002. Rangeland health attributes and indicators for qualitative assessment. Journal of Range Management. 55:584-297.

Rodhouse, T., A. St. John and L. Garrett. 2003. 2002-2003 Vertebrate Inventory Whitman Mission National Historic Site. University of Idaho, Moscow, Idaho 62 pp.

Romo, J. and W. Krueger. 1985. Weed Control and Revegetation Alternatives for Whitman MissionNational Historic Site. Oregon State University, CPSU/OSU 85-9. 56 pp.

Running, S.W., 2006: Is global warming causing more larger wildfires? Science, 313, 927-928.

Seaber, Paul R., F. Paul Kapinos, and George L. Knapp. 1987. Hydrologic Unit Maps. U.S. Geological Survey Water Supply Paper 2294.

Starkey, E. N. 2009. Upper Columbia Basin Network Integrated Water Quality Annual Report 2008: Nez Perce National Historical Park (NEPE) and Whitman Mission National Historic Site (WHMI). DRAFT Natural Resource Technical Report NPS/UCBN/NRTR—2009/xxx. National Park Service, Fort Collins, Colorado.

U.S. Army Corps of Engineers (USACE). 1995. Mill Creek Master Plan - Technical Report: Volume 2. USACE Walla Walla District report. 357pp.

U.S. Census Bureau, 2007, State and County QuickFacts. Online. http://quickfacts.census.gov/qfd/index.html Accessed 1 January 2009.

U.S. Forest Service and U.S. Geological Survey. 2008. LANDFIRE National Data Products. Online. http://www.landfire.gov/products_national.php. Accessed 1 January 2009.

Solutions to Environmental and Economic Problems (STEEP). 2008. PNW Conservation Tillage Handbook.. Washington State University, Oregon State University and University of Idaho. Online. http://pnwsteep.wsu.edu/tillagehandbook/index.htm. Accessed 1 January 2009.

Walla Walla County Board of Commissioners.(WWCBC). 2007. Walla Walla County Comprehensive Plan.Online. http://www.co.walla-walla.wa.us/departments/comdev/WallaWallaCountyComprehensivePlan.shtml. Accessed 1 January 2009.

Washington State Noxious Weed Control Board (WSNWCB). 2009. Washington State Noxious Weed List. Washington State Department of Agriculture. Online. http://www.nwcb.wa.gov/documents/weed%20lists/State%20Weed%20List%202009.pdf . Accessed 1 March 2009.

Westerling, A. L., H. G. Hidalgo, D. R. Cayan, and T. W. Swetnam. 2006. Warming and earlier spring increase western U.S. forest wildfire activity. Science, 313, 940-943.

Western Regional Climate Center. 2003. Washington Climate Summaries. Desert Research Institute, Reno, Nevada. Online. http://www.wrcc.dri.edu/summary/climsmwa.html. Accessed 1 January 2009.

Wissmar, Robert C., Jeanette E. Smith, Bruce A. McIntosh, Hiram W. Li, Gordon H. Reeves, and James R. Sedell. 1994. Ecological health of river basins in forested regions of eastern Washington and Oregon. Gen. Tech. Rep. PNW-GTR-326. Portland, OR: U.S. Department of Agriculture, Forest Service, Pacific Northwest Research Station. 65 p. (Everett, Richard L., assessment team leader; Eastside forest ecosystem health assessment; Hessburg, Paul F., science team leader and tech. ed., Volume III: assessment.)

Appendix A – List of NRCA Geodatabase Data by Theme

Theme	Layer Name
Air Resources	
Animal	
Climate	
Precipitation	Precipitation_1
Temperature	whmi_temp_avg
Geography	
Roads	whmi_roads
Natural Resource Plots	nrca_plots
Park Boundary	whmi_parkbndy
Public Land Survey System WA	PLSS_Wa
Public Land Survey System OR	PLSS_Or
Project Bounday	whmi_projbndy
Cities	whmi_city_bndy
Geology	
Soils-County Surveys	whmi_soils
Geology	whmi_geology
Park Soils	whmi_park_soil
Land_Process	
Landuse	
Plant	
Integrated Pest Management 2002-2005	whmi_ipm_02_05
Vegetation Restoration Management Units	whmi_vrm
Stressors	
Water Resources	
Watershed Basin - 6th HUC	whmi_basins
Streams	streams
Lakes	Water_Bodies
Water (303d listed) Oregon	streams_303d_or
Water (303d listed) Washington	streams_303d_wa
Springs	water_sources
Monitoring Stations	whmi_env_monitoring_stations
Raster Data	
Digital Elevation Model	whmi_dem
Existing Vegetation	whmi_evt
Hillshade	whmi_hlsd
Color Aerial Imagery	whmi_aerial.sid

Appendix B – List of Indicators Analyzed to Calculate Landscape Attribute Values.

Plot No.	VRM Unit	Ecological Reference Code	Soil Name	1. Rills	2. Waterflow	3. Pedestal	4. Bare	5. Gullies	6. Wind	7. Litter	8. Soil Surface	9. Soil Degredation
1	D3	R007XY701WA	UpA - Umapine silt loam	N-S	N-S	N-S	S-M	N-S	N-S	N-S	M-E	S-M
2	D4c	R008XY601WA	CaA - Catherine silt loam	N-S	N-S	N-S	S-M	N-S	N-S	N-S	M	M
3	C1-H3	R008XY103WA	Rlf - Ritsville silt loam	N-S	N-S	N-S	S-M	N-S	N-S	N-S	M	M
4	C1-H6	R008XY102WA	EfB - Ellisforde silt loam	N-S	N-S	N-S	N-S	N-S	N-S	N-S	S-M	S-M
5	B	R009XY401WA	PmA - Pedigo silt loam	N-S	N-S	N-S	N-S	N-S	N-S	N-S	S-M	S-M
6	F2	R009XY401WA	PmA - Pedigo silt loam	N-S	N-S	N-S	N-S	N-S	N-S	N-S	N-S	S-M
7	C2-H5	R008XY103WA	Tc - Terrace escarpments	N-S	N-S	N-S	N-S	N-S	N-S	N-S	S-M	M

Appendix B (continued).

Plot No.	VRM Units	Ecological Reference Code	Soil Name	10. Plant Canopy Cover	11. Compaction	12. Function Structure	13. Plant Mortality	14. Litter Amount	15. Annual Production	16. Invasive Species	17. Reproduction
1	D3	R007XY701WA	UpA - Umapine silt loam	S-M	N-S	S-M	N-S	N-S	N-S	S-M	N-S
2	D4c	R008XY601WA	CaA - Catherine silt loam	S-M	N-S	M	S-M	S-M	M	M	S-M
3	C1-H3	R008XY103WA	Rlf - Ritsville silt loam	M	N-S	M	N-S	N-S	M	M-E	S-M
4	C1-H6	R008XY102WA	EfB - Ellisforde silt loam	N-S	N-S	S-M	S-M	N-S	N-S	N-S	N-S
5	B	R009XY401WA	PmA - Pedigo silt loam	N-S	N-S	E	M	M-E	M	M	M
6	F2	R009XY401WA	PmA - Pedigo silt loam	S-M	N-S	E	N-S	M-E	N-S	M	M
7	C2-H5	R008XY103WA	Tc - Terrace escarpments	M	N-S	M-E	S-M	M	M	E	M

Appendix C List of Plant Species at NRCA Upland Assessment Points

Species Name	Growth Form	Non-Native	Noxious	Aerial Cover by Plot						
				1	2	3	4	5	6	7
Salix lasiandra	tree				60				20	
Populus trichocarpa	tree				30				20	
Robina pseudo-acacia	tree								5	
Chrysothamnus nauseosus	shrub					10				1
Sambucus cerulea	shrub							0.5		
Pseudoroegeneria spicata	grass									
Apera interrupta	grass	X		0.5						
Thinopyrum intermedium	grass	X		30						
Thinopyrum ponticum	grass	X		60				40		
Bromus japonicus	grass	X			20					
Bromus tectorum	grass	X			50	50	10	60		80
Koeleria macrantha	grass				2					
Leymus cinereus	grass					2				
Poa secunda	grass				10					1
Phalaris arundinacea	grass								90	
Achillea millefolium	forb				2	0.5				
Amsinckia lycopsoides	forb				3					
Asparagus officinalis	forb	X			1		1	0.5		
Centaurea solstitialis	forb	X	X		30					10
Cirsium arvense	forb	X	X	0.5	1			0.5		
Cirsium vulgare	forb	X	X				5			
Conium maculatum	forb	X	X		2		1			
Convuvulus arvensis	forb	X	X	5						
Descurainia richardsonii	forb			0.5		5		2		
Dipsacus sylvestris	forb	X			1			2		
Eriogonum niveum	forb			2	1		20			15
Galium aparine	forb	X			25					
Hemizonia pungens	forb	X	X	0.5						
Lactuca serriola	forb	X			0.5			0.5		0.5
Lamium amplixicaule	forb	X		0.5	0.5			0.5		
Lupinus leucophyllus	forb						0.5			

Appendix D: Aquatic Site Properly Functioning Condition Checklists and Invertebrate Site Description Forms

Lotic Standard Checklist

Name of Riparian-Wetland Area: <u>WHMI – Doan Creek</u>

Date: <u>5/13/08</u>   Segment/Reach ID: <u>Restored reach</u>   Acres: _____

ID Team Observers: <u>Hinson, Ladd</u>

Yes	No	N/A	HYDROLOGY
	X		1) Floodplain above bankfull is inundated in "relatively frequent" events
		X	2) Where beaver dams are present they are active and stable
X			3) Sinuosity, width/depth ratio, and gradient are in balance with the landscape setting (i.e., landform, geology, and bioclimatic region)
	X		4) Riparian-wetland area is widening or has achieved potential extent
	X		5) Upland watershed is not contributing to riparian-wetland degradation

Yes	No	N/A	VEGETATION
	X		6) There is diverse age-class distribution of riparian-wetland vegetation (recruitment for maintenance/recovery)
	X		7) There is diverse composition of riparian-wetland vegetation for maintenance/recovery)
X			8) Species present indicate maintenance of riparian-wetland soil moisture characteristics
X			9) Streambank vegetation is comprised of those plants or plant communities that have root masses capable of withstanding high streamflow events
X			10) Riparian-wetland plants exhibit high vigor
	X		11) Adequate riparian-wetland vegetative cover is present to protect banks and dissipate energy during high flows
	X		12) Plant communities are an adequate source of coarse and/or large woody material (for maintenance/recovery)

Yes	No	N/A	EROSION/DEPOSITION
X			13) Floodplain and channel characteristics (i.e., rocks, overflow channels, coarse and/or large woody material) are adequate to dissipate energy
	X		14) Point bars are revegetating with riparian-wetland vegetation
X			15) Lateral stream movement is associated with natural sinuosity
X			16) System is vertically stable
X			17) Stream is in balance with the water and sediment being supplied by the watershed (i.e., no excessive erosion or deposition)

Remarks (numbers correspond to checklist items)

Doan Creek is a spring-fed system and is controlled for irrigation purposes, which results in low frequency of flood events. Flood indicators are not present.

Beaver dams and beaver activity are absent.

Doan Creek has been recently restored and artificially engineered to function appropriately.

Irrigation control activities are currently keeping water out of the channel from approximately mid-May to August.

Re-vegetated channel consists of planted willow stakes and newly emergent herbaceous species.

Planted willow stakes along reach are thriving, which indicates maintenance of soil moisture content.

Willows on stream bank have root masses that are capable of withstanding high streamflow events.

Plants show new vibrant growth and are vigorous in appearance.

Although willow stakes have been planted, they are not dense enough, nor have enough other woody and herbaceous species established themselves at this time.

Newly planted woody species could potentially provide a source of large woody debris, but adequate sources are not currently present.

Engineered placement of large woody debris is adequate to dissipate energy.

Point bars not currently present, likely due to the freshly restored channel that has not had a chance to convey channel-forming flows yet.

Engineered meanders and sinuosity present.

Summary Determination

Functional Rating:

Proper Functioning Condition _____

Functional – At Risk __X__

Nonfunctional _____

Unknown _____

Trend for Functional – At Risk:

Upward __X__

Downward _____

Not Apparent _____

Additional notes:

1. Since this channel is in the process of being restored, it is well on its way to becoming properly functioning. It will need to experience more channel forming flows to transition to a balanced stream capable of processing sediment and dissipating flows.

Are factors contributing to unacceptable conditions outside the control of the manager?

Yes __X__

No _____

If yes, what are those factors?

_X_ Flow regulations   ___ Mining activities   ___ Upstream channel conditions

___ Channelization   ___ Road encroachment   ___ Oil field water discharge

___ Augmented flows   _X_ Other (specify) Recent restoration activities

Lotic Standard Checklist

Name of Riparian-Wetland Area: <u>WHMI – Mill Creek</u>
Date: <u>5/14/08</u>   Segment/Reach ID: <u>Entire reach on NPS property</u> Acres: _____
ID Team Observers: <u>Hinson, Ladd</u>

Yes	No	N/A	HYDROLOGY
	X		1) Floodplain above bankfull is inundated in "relatively frequent" events
		X	2) Where beaver dams are present they are active and stable
X			3) Sinuosity, width/depth ratio, and gradient are in balance with the landscape setting (i.e., landform, geology, and bioclimatic region)
	X		4) Riparian-wetland area is widening or has achieved potential extent
	X		5) Upland watershed is not contributing to riparian-wetland degradation

Yes	No	N/A	VEGETATION
	X		6) There is diverse age-class distribution of riparian-wetland vegetation (recruitment for maintenance/recovery)
	X		7) There is diverse composition of riparian-wetland vegetation for maintenance/recovery)
X			8) Species present indicate maintenance of riparian-wetland soil moisture characteristics
X			9) Streambank vegetation is comprised of those plants or plant communities that have root masses capable of withstanding high streamflow events
X			10) Riparian-wetland plants exhibit high vigor
	X		11) Adequate riparian-wetland vegetative cover is present to protect banks and dissipate energy during high flows
	X		12) Plant communities are an adequate source of coarse and/or large woody material (for maintenance/recovery)

Yes	No	N/A	EROSION/DEPOSITION
	X		13) Floodplain and channel characteristics (i.e., rocks, overflow channels, coarse and/or large woody material) are adequate to dissipate energy
	X		14) Point bars are revegetating with riparian-wetland vegetation
	X		15) Lateral stream movement is associated with natural sinuosity
	X		16) System is vertically stable
X			17) Stream is in balance with the water and sediment being supplied by the watershed (i.e., no excessive erosion or deposition)

Remarks (numbers correspond to checklist items)

1. Channel confinement and channelization present due to farming and railroad bridge crossing at upstream end of reach. Flood indicators are not present.

2. Beaver dams and beaver activity are absent.

4. High banks keep stream from meandering and increasing riparian width; potential exists for much larger riparian with bank setback.

5. Farmland and railroad bed erosion.

6. Well-established older individuals present as well as younger age classes; however middle age classes are absent.

Canarygrass and larger willow/cottonwood species present; need more native diversity.

Willows and cottonwood will withstand high streamflow events.

Greater than 50% of bank not protected by erect woody vegetation.

Not enough sources of large woody debris for channel maintenance.

No floodplain connection or access to LWD outside confined channel.

Point bars small and without established vegetation due to velocities in confined channel.

No lateral movement because the reach is channelized.

Channel confinement causing accelerated downcutting.

Summary Determination

Functional Rating:

Proper Functioning Condition _____

Functional – At Risk __X__

Nonfunctional _____

Unknown _____

Trend for Functional – At Risk:

Upward _____

Downward __X__

Not Apparent _____

Additional notes:

1. Channel confinement (i.e., rip rap) and channelization creates an unnatural system that is not dissipating energy at full potential.

Are factors contributing to unacceptable conditions outside the control of the manager?

Yes __X__

No _____

If yes, what are those factors?

_X_ Flow regulations   ___ Mining activities   ___ Upstream channel conditions

_X_ Channelization   ___ Road encroachment   ___ Oil field water discharge

___ Augmented flows   _X_ Other (specify) Railroad trestle at upstream end of reach

Invertebrate Site Description Form

Name of Riparian-Wetland Area: ____Whitman Mission (WHMI)_____

Date: __5/14/2008_ Segment/Reach ID: _Mill Creek 1_____ Stream: _ Mill Creek _

ID Team Observers: __Hinson, Ladd_____

Stream Channel

Description	Yes/No
Channelized	Y

Stream Substrate and Shoreline Condition

Description	Percent (%)
Inorganic Substrate	95
Organic Substrate	5
Embeddedness	10
Sediment	25-30
Stream Shading	15

Site Measurements

Description	Meters
Stream Width	12.2
Surface Velocity (m/s)	0.8
Water Depth (Average)	0.3
Riffle Length	21.0
Riffle Width (Average)	2.0

NPS 371/100128, June 2009